TOWARD AN ECUMENICAL
FUNDAMENTAL THEOLOGY

American Academy of Religion
Academy Series

edited by
Carl A. Raschke

Number 47

TOWARD AN ECUMENICAL FUNDAMENTAL THEOLOGY

by
Randy L. Maddox

Randy L. Maddox

TOWARD AN ECUMENICAL
FUNDAMENTAL THEOLOGY

Scholars Press
Chico, California

TOWARD AN ECUMENICAL
FUNDAMENTAL THEOLOGY

by
Randy L. Maddox
Ph.D., 1982, Emory University

© 1984
American Academy of Religion

BR118
M33
1984

Library of Congress Cataloging in Publication Data

Maddox, Randy L.
Toward an ecumenical fundamental theology.

(American Academy of Religion academy series ; 47)
Bibliography: p.
Includes index.
1. Theology—Methodology. 2. Theology, Doctrinal.
3. Apologetics—20th century. I. Title. II. Series
BR118.M33   1984   230   84–13838
ISBN 0–89130–771–0

Printed in the United States of America
on acid-free paper

To Aileen

I ask you to receive her in the Lord in a way worthy of the saints and to give her any help she may need from you, for she has been a great help to many people, including me. (Romans 16:2, NIV)

TABLE OF CONTENTS

PREFACE

The paths leading to this project converged from several directions. One of the focus issues of my graduate study was the contemporary discussion of theological method, particularly the encyclopedic aspects of that discussion. I used Gerhard Ebeling as a key dialogue partner in my investigation of these issues because of the direct treatment he gives to the theological role of such subjects as church history, biblical studies and philosophy. It was during my reading of Ebeling that I first encountered the discussion of a Protestant (or ecumenical) fundamental theology.

Another of my interests was to develop a better understanding of Catholic theology. Besides my own reading of such contemporary theologians as Lonergan, Küng, Metz and Schillebeeckx, I am indebted in this regard to Dr. Jeremy Miller, O.P. for instructive seminars on Aquinas and Karl Rahner. These courses proved indispensable for understanding the new trends in the Catholic discussion of fundamental theology.

The decisive stimulus for this project, however, was a course in theological encyclopedia under Dr. Theodore Jennings. Part of the assignment for this course was to develop one's own outline of a theological encyclopedia. It was during the struggle with this assignment that I developed an intense interest in the conception of fundamental theology as a meta-theological discipline concerned with legitimacy in theology per se. The present dissertation is my attempt both to refine this conception of fundamental theology and to gain a perspective on it by comparison with other conceptions.

My indebtedness to Dr. Jennings goes far beyond his guidance in the course on theological method. He has given generously of his time, expertise and encouragement in directing me through the various stages of my graduate program and finally with the dissertation itself. His many helpful criticisms

have served to clarify my thinking even at those points where
we had continuing differences of opinion. A more ideal *Doktor-*
vater is hard to imagine.

Sincere thanks are due as well to the other members of my
committee--Drs. Jack Boozer, Thomas Flynn, Jeremy Miller,
Theodore Runyon and Don Saliers--for their numerous contributions to both this project and my study at Emory as a whole.

Above all, I wish to express publicly my indebtedness and
appreciation to the *sine qua non* of my graduate education,
my wife Aileen. Without her willingness to "put hubby through,"
her ungrudging acceptance of the many hours devoted to study,
and especially her constant encouragement and support, this
project would have been impossible. Hence, the dedication.

ABBREVIATIONS

DS   Denzinger, Heinrich. *Echiridion symbolorum*. Edition 33, edited
          by Adolf Schönmetzer. Barcinone: Herder, 1965.

EKL   *Evangelisches Kirchenlexikon*. 3 vols. Edited by H. Brunotte
          and O. Weber. Göttingen: Vandenhoeck and Ruprecht, 1956-9.

Enc   *Encounter*

EnTh   *Encyclopedia of Theology*. (The Concise *Sacramentum Mundi*).
          Edited by Karl Rahner. New York: Seabury, 1975.

EvTh   *Evangelische Theologie*

FZPhTh   *Freiburger Zeitschrift für Philosophie und Theologie*

HeyJ   *Heythrop Journal*

InKaZ   *Internationale katholische Zeitschrift*

JAAR   *Journal of the American Academy of Religion*

JR   *Journal of Religion*

JThC   *Journal for Theology and Church*

KuD   *Kerygma und Dogma*

LThK²   *Lexikon für Theologie und Kirche*. Second Edition. 10 vols.
          Edited by J. Höfer and K. Rahner. Freiburg: Herder, 1957-65.

MThZ   *Münchener theologische Zeitschrift*

NCE   *New Catholic Encyclopedia*. 17 vols. Edited by W. J. McDonald
          et al. New York: McGraw-Hill, 1967-79.

NZSTh   *Neue Zeitschrift für systematische Theologie*

RelStR   *Religious Studies Review*

RSPhTh   *Revue des Sciences philosophiques et théologique*

RSR   *Recherches de science religieuse*

ThD   *Theology Digest*

ThGl   *Theologie und Glaube*

ThPh   *Theologie und Philosophie*

ThQ   *Theologische Quartelschrift*

ThR   *Theologische Revue*

ThZ   *Theologische Zeitschrift*

TS   *Theological Studies*

TThZ   *Trierer theologische Zeitschrift*

ZThK   *Zeitschrift für Theologie und Kirche*

ZZ   *Zwischen den Zeiten*

INTRODUCTION

One of the safest generalizations concerning contemporary
theological discussion is that problems of methodology have
come to occupy a prominent role. Indeed, one sometimes gets
the impression that all constructive theological proposals have
been put on hold, in lieu of discussion *about* doing theology.
Moreover, this discussion of theological method appears itself
to have reached a stalemate. An important reason for the
present stalemate is that most methodological proposals are of
an ad hoc nature, arising in response to particular issues such
as: "What is the role of historical investigation in theological formulations?" (Harvey); "How can a theologian use the
Bible?" (Kelsey); or "Can theology justify its place as a
'science' in the university?" (Pannenberg). The pressing
problem which faces contemporary theologians is the provision
of an integrative context that would facilitate discussion
between such diverse responses to particular questions so that
their significance for each other can be properly assessed.
Only if and when this is accomplished can we hope to acquire
even a provisional grasp of the role and scope of methodological
questions within the theological enterprise as a whole.

A promising move towards the provision of such a context is
evident in the discussion of an ecumenical fundamental theology.
This discussion is concerned with the development of an interconfessional consensus on the basic task, scope and structure
of a theological discipline which treats questions of the
responsible grounding of Christian faith and/or theology.

It is our contention that a careful consideration of this
discussion has importance and promise, not only for clarifying
the possible role of fundamental theology per se, but even more
for clarification of the role of questions of theological method
within the theological enterprise as a whole. In keeping with
this contention, the purpose of this essay is to provide a

1

presentation and analysis of this interconfessional discussion of fundamental theology in such a way that its ecumenical possibilities and its significance for the wider discussions of theological method can become evident. Three steps will be taken in accomplishing this task. First, a brief history of the development of the discipline of fundamental theology will be given. Second, the present state of the discussion will be illustrated by means of a typology of the alternative under-standings of the task and scope of fundamental theology. Third, we will advance a constructive proposal for understanding the task and scope of an ecumenical fundamental theology in light of the present discussion.

A. *What is "Fundamental Theology"?*

A typical response to the question "What is fundamental theology?" is that of Bouillard: "The term *fundamental theology* . . . designates simultaneously and puts in the same bracket two disciplines that are distinct in their object and method: apologetics . . . and the treatise on the grounds of theology, or sources of theological knowledge."[1] While essentially correct, this definition suffers a critical limitation. For Bouillard the treatise on the grounds of theology is concerned only to "demonstrate how Scripture, Tradition, and the magis-terium witness to divine revelation."[2] As Geffré points out, this is too limited a view. Fundamental theology is not limited merely to reflection on the sources of theology. Rather, it aims at providing the critical function inherent in all scientific activity--i.e., that of explaining the basis *and method* of the science of theology.[3] While questions about the proper sources of theology would be an essential part of this critical endeavor, they must be supplemented by such questions as those of the proper use of language, research methodologies and argument that have been a focus of recent discussions of theological method.

Thus, fundamental theology is typically understood as a discipline which deals with questions both of the responsible justification of Christian faith (apologetics) and the methodological justification of Christian theology. Now, apologetics is usually understood as the philosophical defense

of central Christian notions such as God, Christ and the Church,
in the face of external attacks upon them. By contrast, questions of theological method are usually understood to deal with
procedural matters such as: "How does tradition function as
a norm for constructing a doctrine?"; or "How should one
structure a dogmatics?" On first consideration the incorporation of two such apparently disparate activities into a single
discipline seems purely arbitrary and not conducive to meaningful discussion.

Two points should be noted in this regard. First, one of
the tasks of our historical investigation will be to show how
this association grew out of the "logic" of the inquiry into
these issues during the last two centuries. In an age when a
critically oriented philosophy replaced a metaphysically oriented
one, it became evident that the task of giving a responsible
justification for Christian faith entailed the task of critically
justifying the sources and methods used to bring that faith to
self-understanding. The link between these two tasks is their
common question of truth. As Ted Peters summarizes this point:
"If the proper 'road' or 'way' to ultimate truth (i.e., theological method) becomes available, then the apologetic task
will have been all but completed."[4]

At the same time, both our historical summary and our
typological overview of the various contemporary understandings
of fundamental theology will reveal that there remain some
unresolved tensions between formulations of fundamental theology
aimed more at apologetics and those aimed more at considerations
of theological method. One of the central tasks of our constructive proposal for fundamental theology will be to suggest
a solution to these tensions.

B. *The Interconfessional Character of the Current Discussion*

To anyone acquainted with the history of interconfessional
dialogue, the present attempt to develop an ecumenical fundamental theology must seem, at best, surprising and, at worst,
sensationalism;[5] for, until about a decade ago, there was an
apparent interconfessional agreement that fundamental theology
was a uniquely Catholic discipline.

This can be illustrated first on the Protestant side. Until recently, the term "fundamental theology" almost never appeared in Protestant dogmatic texts or theological encyclopedias; and when it did, it was referred to as a Catholic discipline.[6] More importantly, Protestants not only avoided the name "fundamental theology"; influential Protestants also rejected what they understood to be the task of fundamental theology. For example, Barth rejected any attempt to "analyse man in the light of divine revelation from creation as the *introitus* to the inner circle of true theology grounded in a *revelatio specialis*" as being a task that was "only possible in the realm of Roman Catholicism."[7]

This viewpoint was confirmed on the Catholic side. In 1954 we find Heinrich Fries stating that "Protestant theology not only is not acquainted with the inquiry of Catholic fundamental theology, but avoids it on principle."[8] This opinion could be reaffirmed as recently as 1969.[9]

However, a breakdown in this restriction of fundamental theology to the side of Catholicism is rapidly becoming apparent. Not only are Protestant theologians beginning to use the term "fundamental theology" and to deepen their concern for the tasks normally associated with it; Catholic theologians, for their part, are welcoming this change as having significant ecumenical promise.

The ground-breaking work, in this regard, was Gerhard Ebeling's "Erwägungen zu einer evangelischen Fundamental-theologie" which appeared in 1970.[10] In this article Ebeling argued that while Protestant theologians may not use the term "fundamental theology," they did, in fact, engage many of the tasks of this discipline under other names such as apologetics and theological encyclopedia (pp. 483-84). Further, he defended the startling thesis that the origin of the name "fundamental theology" as the designation of a discipline in Catholic theology had been significantly influenced by then contemporary Protestant theological linguistic practice (p. 505). Since Ebeling's article, other Protestant theologians such as W. Pannenberg, R. Hart, L. Gilkey, P. Hodgson and E. Farley have begun to use this terminology as an explicit designation for activities carried on by Protestant theologians.

Rather than reacting to this acceptance of the name and concerns of fundamental theology by Protestants with cries of "Encroachment!" or "Obfuscation!", the typical Catholic response has been favorable. Indeed, Heinrich Fries has recently argued that discussion of the possibilities of an ecumenical fundamental theology represents the best, if not the only, means of over-coming the widespread deadlock in ecumenical dialogue.[11] More recently, Harold Wagner has argued that the discussion has advanced to the point that fundamental theology is now essentially ecumenical in its basic structure.[12]

The rather optimistic opinion just noted should not, however, lead to the conclusion that a general agreement on the task and scope of an ecumenical fundamental theology has been reached. The ecumenical unity that has been achieved relative to funda-mental theology is a "working unity." That is, it has been agreed that the most fruitful way to pursue a greater agreement about the task, scope and structure of fundamental theology is through interconfessional dialogue. It is important to note that the goal of this dialogue is *not* primarily to overcome differences between a Catholic and a Protestant understanding of fundamental theology but rather to attempt to bridge the gap between different understandings of the discipline found jointly within both confessions.

The situation is hardly that of Catholic theologians having a unanimously accepted understanding of fundamental theology that they now merely need to convey to Protestants. Rather, the question of the task and scope of fundamental theology has been the focus of intense discussion and reformulation even within Catholic circles. Over a decade ago, Joseph Cahill could assert—after investigating thirty-two fundamental theologies—that there was no general Catholic consensus as to the nature and properties of the discipline.[13] If anything, the situation is more complex today since recent discussion has included several innovative proposals for the reformulation of the discipline. Thus, it is not surprising that the Catholic fundamental theologian Josef Schmitz recently characterized his discipline as having a sign hung over its door that read "Temporarily Closed due to Total Reconstruction."[14]

The situation is even more confused on the Protestant side since the discussion is at such a nascent stage. A good way to gain an appreciation for the variety of understandings of the task and scope of fundamental theology among Protestants is to review the diverse traditional Protestant activities that have been identified, in part or in whole, with fundamental theology. Besides apologetics and theological encyclopedia already mentioned by Ebeling, these include prolegomena to dogmatics (*Prinzipienlehre*), natural theology or philosophical theology, hermeneutical theory, philosophy of science (*Wissen-schaftstheorie*), metatheory of theology, and even theology of culture.[15] Obviously, diverse understandings of the task and scope of fundamental theology lie behind such diverse determinations of its analogues.

In short, while the discussion of the nature of fundamental theology has made a significant advance in the last decade by becoming a truly interconfessional discussion, it is still far removed from the goal of an ecumenical agreement concerning the task, scope and structure of the discipline. A major obstacle to such an agreement is the lack of an investigation of the interrelationships of the numerous recent attempts to reformulate fundamental theology. Such an investigation is an indispensable prerequisite to any significant advance in the discussion, and the central part of this essay will be devoted to just such an investigation. Following a brief history of the discipline of fundamental theology (part one), we will present a typology of the present discussion of the task and scope of fundamental theology (part two). Finally, in light of this typology, we will advance our own proposal for understanding fundamental theology (part three).

---

[1]Henri Bouillard, "Human Experience as the Starting Point of Fundamental Theology," *Concilium* 6 (1965): 79.

[2]Ibid., p. 80.

[3]Claude Geffré, "Recent Developments in Fundamental Theology: An Interpretation," *Concilium* 46 (1969): 5-6.

[4]Ted Peters, "Truth in History: Gadamer's Hermeneutic and Pannenberg's Apologetics," JR 55 (1975): 36-37.

[5]See Ebeling's sensitivity to this charge in "Erwägungen zu einer evangelischen Fundamentaltheologie," ZThK 67 (1970): 479.

[6]For example, one of the few articles to be found on this topic is a brief one in the *Evangelische Kirchenlexikon* which states explicitly: "Fundamental theology, also called *apologetics*, is a basic discipline of Roman Catholic theology." K. Nitzsche, "Fundamentaltheologie," EKL I, 1408.

[7]Karl Barth. *Church Dogmatics*, (Edinburgh: T & T Clark, 1975), I:1: 130. N.B., while all translation in this project will be rendered in inclusive language unless this contradicts the apparent intention of the author, the integrity of English quotations has been respected for purposes of accuracy.

[8]Heinrich Fries, "Eine neue Fundamentaltheologie," ThQ 134 (1954): 470.

[9]See Josef Schmitz. "Die Fundamentaltheologie im 20. Jahrhundert," in *Bilanz der Theologie im 20. Jahrhundert*, ed. H. Vorgrimler and R. Vander Gucht (Freiburg: Herder, 1969), p. 230.

[10]ZThK 67 (1970): 479-524.

[11]Heinrich Fries, "Die ökumenische Dimension der Fundamentaltheologie," *Ökumenische Rundschau* 22 (1973): 224.

[12]Harald Wagner, "Evangelische Fundamentaltheologie," *Catholica* 31 (1977): 26.

[13]Joseph Cahill, "A Fundamental Theology of Our Time," *Concilium* 46 (1969): 93.

[14]Quoted in F. Hahn, "Exegese und Fundamentaltheologie," ThQ 155 (1975): 263.

[15]See respectively: Wilfried Joest, *Fundamentaltheologie. Theologische Grundlagen und Methodenprobleme*, (Stuttgart: Kohlhammer, 1974), p. 9; John Macquarrie, *Principles of Christian Theology*, (NY: Scribner's, 1966), p. 39; Elisabeth Gößmann, "Fundamentaltheologie und Apologetik," in *Was ist Theologie?* ed. E. Neuhäusler and E. Gößmann (Munich: Max Heuber Verlag, 1966), p. 33; Max Seckler, "Evangelische Fundamentaltheologie. Zu einem Novum aus katholischer Sicht," ThQ 155 (1975): 292; Gerhard Sauter *et al., Grundlagen der Theologie--ein Diskurs*, (Stuttgart: Kohlhammer, 1974), p. 67; and Ray Hart, *Unfinished Man and the Imagination*, (NY: Seabury, 1968), p. 14.

PART ONE

HISTORICAL BACKGROUND TO THE
CONTEMPORARY DISCUSSION

INTRODUCTION

Our first major task in this essay is to gain a historical overview of the discipline of fundamental theology. One question for this overview will be the identification of distinct confessional stances towards the discipline. If we are to develop an *ecumenical* fundamental theology, then we must gain an understanding of the historical precedents for such an enterprise.

Another question for the overview will be the association of considerations of apologetics and questions of theological method in the discipline of fundamental theology. In particular, the alternatives regarding this association will be noted and an attempt to clarify the "logic" of the association will be made.

These two questions ultimately converge because one of the characteristics of the confessional orientation towards fundamental theology is that there have been distinct Protestant and Catholic views regarding the primacy of apologetic and methodological formulations of fundamental theology. It is precisely this situation that will set the stage for our subsequent discussion of the characteristics of an *ecumenical* fundamental theology.

The organization of this historical overview is suggested by two significant results of the recent interconfessional discussion of fundamental theology. First, it has become evident that the tendency to see this discipline as distinctively Catholic did not characterize it at its inception. Indeed, Protestant theologians contributed significantly to the creation of the discipline. It was only after the middle of the nineteenth century that the interconfessional opposition concerning fundamental theology became pronounced. Second, it has also become evident that this recent interconfessional discussion of fundamental theology was not entirely fortuitous. There

11

were significant interconfessional developments that prepared
the way for the discussion.

In light of these realizations, we will structure the
historical overview in three chapters dealing with 1) The
Transconfessional Origins of Fundamental Theology, 2) The Interconfessional Opposition Over Fundamental Theology, and 3) The
Interconfessional Dialogue About Fundamental Theology. In these
sections our focus will be on the possibility and task of a
fundamental theology, not on particular answers to fundamental-
theological issues.

CHAPTER ONE
TRANSCONFESSIONAL ORIGINS OF
FUNDAMENTAL THEOLOGY

Fundamental theology developed as an explicit discipline in
the context of the Enlightenment. It did not, however, develop
ex nihilo. Rather, it inherited activities which were already
present in the life of the Church and adapted them to its unique
purposes. Moreover, this very adaptation was motivated by
rival conceptions of these activities which also contributed,
thereby, to the background of the development of fundamental
theology. Accordingly, before surveying the earliest uses of
"fundamental theology," we must consider briefly the background
for these uses.

A. *Background for Development of Fundamental Theology*

Two traditional theological activities that contributed
directly to the development of fundamental theology were apologetic defenses of the faith and methodological reflections
on the explication of the faith.

1. Apologetics

While the isolation of a particular discipline of apologetics
did not occur until the late eighteenth century,[1] the apologetic
enterprise--as the attempt to explain and defend the Christian
faith in the presence of nonbelievers--has been present in the
Christian Church since its inception.[2] We cannot enter into an
extensive historical consideration of this enterprise. However,
it is important, relative to the development of fundamental
theology, to note the classical (Scholastic--both Catholic and
Protestant) form this enterprise took in the early Enlightenment
setting. Two significant forces shaped the apologetic endeavors
of this time. First, there was a growing cleavage between the
natural reality of human thought and life and the sphere of

grace, revelation and faith. Hence, the need arose to find a bridge between the two worlds. In particular, there was the need to show the necessity of the "religious" world for the "natural" world. Second, the division within the Church at the Reformation made it necessary to present not only defenses against non-Christians, but also a defense for a particular type of Christian belief.

In light of these forces, theologians developed the classical three-step apologetics. The earliest example of this structure is P. Charron's *Les troes vérités contra les athées, les idolâtres, juifs, mohométans, hérétiques et schismatiques* (1593). These three steps became known in Catholic circles as *demonstratio religiosa* which argued for a belief in God and the value of religion against the atheists; *demonstratio christiana* which defended the need for and validity of the special revelation found in Jesus Christ against the Deists and non-Christian religions; and *demonstratio catholica* which argued for the unique validity of the Catholic Church as the deposit and guardian of the special revelation against heretics and schismatics (including, of course, the Protestants). Protestant apologetics developed along the same structure though, of course, the last step was a *demonstratio protest-antica*.[3]

It is not only the structure of this Scholastic apologetics that is significant. Attention should also be paid to the type of argumentation that was normally employed. The primary attack of Enlightenment thinkers on Christian faith was based on the positive sciences, especially history, and on a subject-centered philosophical system--e.g., Descartes and Kant. The apologists of the Church--both Protestant and Catholic--responded in kind. The dominant tendency was to form a scientific apologetic which, abandoning the point of view of faith, took "natural" philosophical, scientific and historical data as its point of departure and attempted on a purely rational basis to present convincing proof of the possibility and the fact of Christian revelation.[4] The earliest formulations of fundamental theology were associated with alternatives to this Scholastic model.

2.   Theological Method

   While it is true that a preoccupation with questions of
theological method is a characteristic of the modern age for
which no extensive analogue can be found in earlier Christian
history, this should not mislead us into the assumption that
such questions were never previously raised.   On the contrary,
treatments of questions of method can be traced back almost as
far as examples of apologetics.   In Christian antiquity,
significant attempts at a doctrine of theological method can
be seen in Origen's *De principiis*--especially the introduction;
the remarks of Clement of Alexandria on the relationship of
philosophy and revelation, or faith and gnosis; and Augustine's
De doctrina christiana.   From the Middle Ages, one could refer
especially to the treatise on theological method of William
of Auxerre.[5]   The issues dealt with in such treatises played
a constituent role in the early formulations of fundamental
theology.

B.   *The Earliest Uses of "Fundamental Theology"*

   In light of the common assumption that fundamental theology
has been traditionally a distinctive Catholic discipline, one
of the surprising discoveries that has surfaced in the recent
investigation of the roots of the discipline is its interconfessional origins.   In fact, the first theologians to use the
term were Protestants.   Moreover, the earliest Catholic uses
of the term and understandings of its task appear to have been
influenced by this Protestant usage.[6]   Our survey of the early
uses of "fundamental theology" will follow this basic historical
order.

1. Protestant Origins

   The earliest known reference to fundamental theology is
found in the Protestant Petrus Annatus in his *Apparatus ad
positivam theologiam Methodicus* (1700).   It is characteristic
of this first stage of the development that Annatus notes the
widespread use of the term to describe positive theology--i.e.,
exegetical theology or the collection of theological data from
its sources.[7]   This understanding of "fundamental" was

developed within the history of the Protestant *Prinzipien-*
lehre (Prolegomena or theological doctrine of principles). This
section of a Protestant dogmatics was devoted primarily to
questions of the sources of theology. It is likely that the
switch from the academic term "principle" to the biblical idea
of "fundament" was facilitated by reference to texts such as
Ephesians 2:20.[8] Indeed, Johann Gerhard explicitly draws the
comparison of "principle" and "fundament."[9]

At its first stage then, fundamental theology referred primarily to the doctrine of the (biblical) sources of theology.
The intriguing aspect about this is that the same concern was
also called "apologetics" by several theologians. To explain
this, as well as to show the continuing development of fundamental
theology, it will be helpful to note how one particular Protestant
faculty--the Tübingen school--incorporated both of these terms.[10]

The Tübingen school can be credited with developing the
Prinzipienlehre into a discipline in its own right. Gottlieb
Storr, the founder of the school, devotes the first section of
his dogmatics to an apology for the appropriation of the biblical
point of view.[11] Gottlieb Planck, his student, was no doubt
motivated by this--in his theological encyclopedia[12]--to preface
exegetical theology (as contrasted with systematic and historical
theology) with a separate discipline which he called *apologetics*:
this was for him the *study of the proofs for the divine origin*
of the doctrines of Scripture. It should be noted that while
apologetic endeavors have been present throughout the history
of the Church, this encyclopedic isolation of a particular
discipline of apologetics is something new with Planck.[13]
Characteristically, he understood apologetics as part of
biblical-exegetical theology.

The final step in the development of the Tübingen school was
taken by Johann Kleuker who explicitly named the collection of
exegetical and apologetic disciplines a "fundamental theology."[14]
He appears to be the first one to apply this title to the
precise task of the exegetical-apologetic grounding of
theology.[15]

We have thus arrived at the point where "fundamental theology"
is used within theology as a designation of a specific discipline.
Significantly, this designation was practically identical with

the term "apologetics." The importance of this fact is that it
sets the stage for the formulation of an alternative conception
of the task of fundamental theology under the influence of
Friedrich Schleiermacher. This alternative formulation was
to become the predominate Protestant understanding of the
discipline during this early period.

While Schleiermacher did not use the precise term "fundamental
theology," he did give lectures on Fundamental Doctrine (i.e.,
Prinzipienlehre) during his teaching activity at Halle (1804).[16]
His real contribution to the question of fundamental theology,
however, is to be found in his definition of the task of philosophical theology. According to Schleiermacher's distinctive
use of the term, philosophical theology is composed of apologetics and polemics. Thus, it deals with the same concerns
which Kleuker treated under fundamental theology--the grounding
of Christian conviction and theology. The uniqueness of
Schleiermacher lies in what he conceives to be the best means
for this grounding. For him, the foundation for the task of
communicating conviction about the truth of the Christian mode
of faith is "formed by investigations concerning the distinctive
nature of Christianity."[17] That is, the proper method of
apologetics is not an external argument about the truth of
Scripture or the miracles of Jesus but rather the critical
demonstration of the essence of contemporary Christianity. As
Ebeling points out, this conception of apologetics involves a
total reconception of the *Prinzipienlehre*. The starting point
for theology is no longer the establishment of the authority
of Scripture but rather the explication of the essence of
Christianity.[18] For later theologians who incorporated
Schleiermacher's understanding of apologetics, fundamental
theology would no longer be an exegetical/apologetic discipline;
it would be a phenomenological/hermeneutic one.

A Protestant approach that was basically in keeping with
Schleiermacher, while explicitly using the term "fundamental
theology," can be found in the theological encyclopedia of
Anton Pelt.[19] Pelt had correctly realized that the recent
developments in the discipline of apologetics--both at Tübingen
and with Schleiermacher--were aimed at understanding this
discipline as a *Prinzipienlehre*.[20] To reflect this new

orientation, he exchanged Schleiermacher's term "apologetics" for "fundamental theology." In Pelt's encyclopedia, fundamental theology became the first part of systematic theology (as distinguished from historical and practical theology). Its task was defined as follows: "Through critical consideration of that which historical theology has determined as uniquely Christian, the essence of Christianity is developed as a foundation for the whole Kingdom of God."[21] On the basis of the principles acquired in this fundamental theology, a system of propositional theology is constructed and its relation to general human knowledge is investigated in a philosophy of Christianity (the other two parts of systematic theology).[22] With Pelt we see again a matter-of-course use of the term "fundamental theology" in the Protestant realm. More importantly, we see that this term had more than one meaning in the theological circles of that day. Kleuker had used it to designate a discipline that grounds theology by giving a rational and historical apology for theology's sources. Pelt, on the other hand, used it to designate a historico-phenomenological analysis of Christianity that was to provide a basis for the whole of Christian life and thought. Both approaches had significant differences from the traditional Scholastic apologetics. The second approach, in particular, should be seen as offering an alternative way of grounding faith in light of the challenge posed by the Enlightenment.

2. Catholic Origins

The traditional Scholastic approach to grounding faith was the dominant form of apologetics in Catholic theology during the early post-Enlightenment. However, there were alternative Catholic understandings of apologetics during this time. In particular, there were understandings which evidenced the influence of Schleiermacher and found their paradigmatic representatives in the Catholic faculty at Tübingen. Significantly, it was in conjunction with these alternative understandings of apologetics that the earliest Catholic uses of "fundamental theology" arose. This leads to the suggestion that the earliest Catholic uses of the term "fundamental theology" and their understanding of the task of fundamental theology were significantly influenced by contemporary Protestant uses of this term.

As with the Protestants, the key developments in the Catholic understanding of fundamental theology were found in the Catholic faculty of the Tübingen school. As Metz points out, the Tübingen school has to be regarded as an exception to the general pattern of apologetics in the Catholic Church during the nineteenth century.[23] Characteristic of this school was a sensitivity to the intelligibility of history, tradition and community to which the more traditional approaches were almost blind.[24] The Tübingen school also manifested a more fruitful interrelationship with Protestant theology and modern thought as a whole than was the case elsewhere.

Johann Sebastian von Drey was the founder of the Catholic Tübingen school. He was professor of apologetics and dogmatic theology at Ellwangen until 1817, when the faculty was transferred to the university at Tübingen, where he continued to teach until 1846.[25] What made Drey so influential on the development of the Tübingen school was his formulation of a new and powerful theological method that could meet the challenges of Kantian and post-Kantian philosophy. The method achieved this end by drawing on Idealism (Schelling) to develop an approach that united history and scientific system, philosophy and theology, in a radically different way than Scholasticism.[26] Drey's method involved a conception of history as having its own ideal necessity. Theology then became essentially a philosophy of historical Christian revelation. In line with this, in his *Kurze Einleitung in das Studium der Theologie* (1819), he divided theology into two basic disciplines-- historical and dogmatic theology. The former established the factualness of the historical content of Catholic tradition; the latter sought to grasp the ideal essences present in this content.[27] Most important for our purposes, however, was the relation between these two disciplines and Drey's understanding of apologetics--as found in his three-volume *Apologetik* (1834-47). Apologetics was not simply a part of dogmatic theology. It was a discipline in its own right. Its aim was not to give a philosophical vindication of God's essence and attributes as the Scholastic apologists had done. For Drey, as a traditionalist,

this was impossible because knowledge was something received
through historical and cultural appropriation, not rational
argumentation. In this light, apologetics was concerned instead
to give a demonstration of Christianity as *the* tradition which
gives the authentic historical expression of God's revelation
and of Catholicism as *the* concrete community that bears this
tradition.[28] What is particularly significant is that apologetics does not effect this demonstration by external arguments
but rather by a manifestation of the Christian religion itself.
As Wagner notes, this understanding of the task and method of
apologetics was, to a large degree, taken over from, or at least
inspired by, Schleiermacher. The significance of this is that
Wagner also considers Drey's *Apologetik* to be the pioneer work
of the new Catholic fundamental theology.[29]

The basic approach of the Tübingen school was formulated into
a developed theological encyclopedia by Drey's student Friedrich
Staudenmaier.[30] The same basic understanding of the method of
apologetics underlies this work as can be seen from Staudenmaier's
assertion that: "The unhindered self-presentation of its spirit
is the one true apologetic of Christianity."[31] The significant
development in Staudenmaier is his encyclopedic placement and
designation of this apologetic task.[32] Having distinguished
between speculative, practical and historical theology; he
proceeds to divide speculative theology into two parts--a
"Theory of Religion and Revelation" and "Dogmatics" proper.
The theory of religion and revelation provides the apologetic
base for dogmatics by demonstrating both the possibility of a
supernatural revelation and the actual expression of that
revelation in Catholicism. It is crucial to notice here in
Staudenmaier a move away from the designation "apologetics"
which is paralleled by a closer affiliation (than Drey, for
example) between his foundational discipline and dogmatics. It
is our contention that these two moves are intimately related
and signal the beginning of the Catholic appropriation of
"fundamental theology." This can best be illustrated by turning
now to the first clear Catholic use of this title.

While there is a possible use of a cognate of "fundamental
theology" in the Catholic realm as early as 1837,[33] the first
clear use of the term is associated with the teaching activity

of the Austrian Johann Nepomuk Ehrlich. In 1856 he occupied
the first established university chair of fundamental theology
at Prague, and in 1859 he published a two-volume work entitled
Fundamentaltheologie.[34] This appears to be the first independent
work with this title by either Protestants or Catholics.[35] It
is significant that Ehrlich inherited his understanding of the
encyclopedic structure of theology from Staudenmaier.[36] He
follows Staudenmaier in distinguishing within doctrinal theology
(Staudenmaier's speculative theology) between dogmatics proper
and a preceding discipline that grounds this dogmatics. However,
instead of calling it "Theory of Religion and Revelation,"
Ehrlich entitles it "Fundamental Theology."[37] Ehrlich mentions
that apologetics is another common designation for this concern;
however, he argues that the two concepts are not identical
because apologetics can be treated as a totally independent
discipline (as in Drey), while fundamental theology is always
coordinated with dogmatics.[38] Here is made explicit an association which was only implicit in Staudenmaier: namely, the
recognition of the necessary close relationship between the
foundation discipline and dogmatics contributed to the dis-
satisfaction with the designation "apologetics" and the
appropriation of a new and more integral designation. That the
term Ehrlich chose--fundamental theology--was not currently
prevalent is obvious in that he felt it necessary to assure the
reader that this was "in no way a new name."[39] He does not
himself give any explicit references to previous uses of the
name. However, we have shown that it had been used in much the
same sense by the Protestant Pelt some fifteen years earlier.
Clear precedents in the Catholic realm are (to our knowledge)
lacking. Thus, it seems reasonable to assume some direct
Protestant influence in Ehrlich's adoption of this term. The
important point is that Ehrlich's appropriation of the term
"fundamental theology" suggests his recognition that his
approach to apologetics is more in line with the "Schleier-
macherian" flavor of Pelt's fundamental theology than with
Scholastic apologetics.

3. Attention to Theological Method

The focus of our reflections so far has been on the apologetic task of fundamental theology. For some of its early
representatives, questions of theological method played only
a small part in this discipline. However, there are significant
indications of a developing awareness of the integral part that
questions of theological method play in establishing Christian
faith and theology. Among these indications is the fact that
fundamental theology developed out of the Protestant *Prinzipienlehre*, which dealt explicitly with the question of the proper
sources of theology. Likewise, the consideration of the
interrelationship of the various theological disciplines--i.e.,
a theological encyclopedia--was integral to the content and
development of fundamental theology. Thus, it was not at all
surprising that Ehrlich began his *Fundamentaltheologie* with an
"Introduction to the Science of Theology."[40] This awareness of
the centrality of questions of theological method to the task
of fundamental theology was to increase significantly as the
discipline developed.

C. *Summary: Characteristics of the Early Discussion*

There were two characteristics of the early developments of
fundamental theology which require emphasis. First, a significant motivation behind the earliest formulations of the
discipline was the need to develop an alternative response to
the challenge of the Enlightenment capable of overcoming the
limitations of the Scholastic apologetics. In particular, the
early formulations of fundamental theology turned to Schleiermacher's phenomenological/hermeneutic approach to apologetics
in order to provide a secure foundation for Christian life
and thought.

This suggests the second characteristic of these early
developments--namely, their transconfessional nature. In their
search for more adequate responses to the Enlightenment, both
Protestant and Catholic theologians--particularly in Tübingen--
found closer allies in like-minded persons of the alternative
confessions than in the Scholastic tradition of their own
confession. That is, the motives and patterns for formulating

the earliest explicit fundamental theologies were not related
to an *inter*confessional dispute. Rather, they were related to
an *intra*confessional dispute over the most effective means of
grounding faith and theology--a dispute that had *trans*confessional importance and representation.

These two characteristics are not just important in helping
us understand the earliest formulations of fundamental theology.
They also help explain how a discipline that arose in such a
transconfessional setting could soon become the locus of interconfessional opposition. Put briefly, the breakdown in the
interconfessional discussion of fundamental theology is
intimately tied to the post-Vatican I Catholic linguistic
shift whereby "fundamental theology" came to be identified with
Scholastic apologetics instead of designating an alternative
to the latter. This shift and its results are the focus of
the next chapter.

[1] See below, p. 16.

[2] The best history of apologetics in English is Avery Dulles, *A History
of Apologetics*, (Phil.: Westminster, 1971).

[3] An informative example of Protestant apologetics is Hugo Grotius,
The Truth of the Christian Religion, trans. John Clarke (London, 1829).

[4] Louis Monden, *Faith: Can Man Still Believe?* (NY: Sheed & Ward,
1970), p. 7.

[5] *Summa Aurea*, ed. Pigouchet (Paris, 1500), cited in Gößmann, "Fundamentaltheologie," p. 26.

[6] As Ebeling properly notes, the importance of such observations is not
to establish confessional claims to priority but rather to justify interconfessional discussion of fundamental theology by showing that both the
subject matter and the terminology were once familiar to Protestants.
Ebeling, "Fundamentaltheologie," p. 505. Our summary of the Protestant
origins of fundamental theology will draw heavily on Ebeling's article.

[7] P. 8 of the Erfurt edition, cited in Wolfhart Pannenberg, *Theology
and the Philosophy of Science*, (Phil.: Westminster, 1976), p. 417fn794.

[8] *superaedificati super fundamentum apostolorum et Prophetarum, etc.*
(Built on the foundation of the apostles and prophets, etc.).

[9] *"Principium primum non habet aliquid prius et fundamentum non fundatur
in alio."* In J. Gerhard, *Loci theologici*, ed. Eduard Preuss (1893), p. 41;
cited in Ebeling, "Fundamentaltheologie," p. 504.

[10] This summary is based on A. F. L. Pelt, *Theologische Encyklopädie
als System im Ausammenhange mit der Geschichte der theologischen Wissenschaft und ihrer einzelnen Zweige entwickelt*, (1845), p. 395; cited in

Ebeling, "Fundamentaltheologie," p. 503fn60.

[11]*Doctrinae christianae pars theoretica e sacris litteris repetita* (1793).

[12]*Einleitung in die theologische {sic} Wissenschaften*, (I, 1794; II, 1795).

[13]Ebeling, "Fundamentaltheologie," p. 491.

[14]See J. Fr. Kleuker, *Grundriss einer Encyklopädie der Theologie*, (1800/01); summarized in Ibid., p. 503fn60.

[15]Ibid. Annatus had merely talked of an identification of fundamental theology with positive theology.

[16]See references in Ebeling, "Fundamentaltheologie," p. 503fn61.

[17]Friedrich Schleiermacher, *Brief Outline of the Study of Theology*, trans. T. Tice (Richmond, VA: John Knox, 1966), p. 31.

[18]Ebeling, "Fundamentaltheologie," p. 494.

[19]A. F. L. Pelt, *Theologische Encyklopädie*.

[20]Ibid., p. 404.

[21]Ibid., p. 371; cited in Ebeling, "Fundamentaltheologie," p. 502.

[22]Ibid.; see a summary of Pelt's system in Ebeling, "Fundamentaltheologie," p. 502fn56.

[23]J. B. Metz, *Faith in History and Society*, (NY: Seabury, 1980), pp. 16-17.

[24]Gerald McCool, *Catholic Theology in the Nineteenth Century*, (NY: Seabury, 1977), p. 13.

[25]A good English summary of Drey's thought can be found in McCool, *Nineteenth Century*, pp. 67-81.

[26]Ibid., p. 68.

[27]Ibid., p. 77.

[28]Ibid., p. 78.

[29]Wagner, "Fundamentaltheologie," p. 20.

[30]*Encyklopädie der theologischen Wissenschaften als System der gesammten Theologie*, (1834).

[31]Ibid., p. 75; cited in Ebeling, "Fundamentaltheologie," p. 494.

[32]Summarized in Ebeling, "Fundamentaltheologie," pp. 499-500.

[33]See Johannes Flury, "Was ist Fundamentaltheologie?" ThZ 31 (1975): 351fn4, for a discussion of the third edition of Friedrich Brenner's *System der katholischen speculativen Theologie*. The fluctuation of Brenner's choice of titles between editions and the unavailability of a copy of the work to investigate its understanding of the task and goal of the second volume limited the usability of this source in the present project.

[34](Prague, 1859-62). On Ehrlich see the dissertation by Erwin Mann, *Idee und Wirklichkeit der Offenbarung. Method und Aufbau der Fundamentaltheologie des Güntherianers J. N. Ehrlich*, (Vienna: Verband der wissenschaften Gesellschaften Österreichs, 1977).

[35]Ebeling, "Fundamentaltheologie," p. 498. Remember, the earlier references were to subsections of theological encyclopedias.

[36]Ehrlich, *Fundamentaltheologie*, I:6, 18.

[37]A detailed comparison of Staudenmaier and Ehrlich can be found in Ebeling, "Fundamentaltheologie," pp. 499-500. The table of contents of Ehrlich's work is reproduced in Stirnimann, "Fundamentaltheologie," p. 294fn12.

[38]Ehrlich, *Fundamentaltheologie*, I:23-24; cited in Ebeling, "Fundamentaltheologie," p. 501fn52.

[39]Ibid., I:22; cited in Ebeling, "Fundamentaltheologie," p. 501fn53.

[40]Ibid., secs. 1-38; cf. Heinrich Stirnimann, "Erwägungen zur Fundamentaltheologie. Problematic, Grundfragen, Konzept," FZPhTh 24 (1977): 291-365.

CHAPTER TWO
INTERCONFESSIONAL OPPOSITION OVER
FUNDAMENTAL THEOLOGY

In this chapter it will be our task to provide a brief account
of the developments that led away from the transconfessional
setting of the origins of fundamental theology and toward the
interconfessional opposition over the possibility and task of
fundamental theology that has characterized modern theological
discussion until the last decade.

In brief, we will try to show how fundamental theology came
to be seen as an exclusively Catholic discipline because of
1) a certain constriction of Catholic expressions through
Vatican I which gave the impression that "fundamental theology"
referred solely to the rational (Scholastic) grounding of faith;
and 2) the opposite Protestant movement, epitomized in Karl
Barth's dialectical theology, of emphasizing the paradoxical
nature of faith.[1]

Our survey of these developments will begin with the Catholic
side since the Protestant developments were, to a significant
degree, reactions against the former.

A. *Catholic Developments: Vatican I*

During the period of Catholic theology when the earliest
formulations of "fundamental theology" developed, there was no
single "established" theological approach. Scholasticism,
which had exercised that function for several centuries, had
been significantly weakened by the suppression of its most
influential supporter--the Society of Jesus--in 1773. As a
result, when Catholic theology was confronted with the rationalism of the Enlightenment, there arose at least three different
types of response.[2] The first of these was the essentially
negative approach of Traditionalism, which asserted that
unaided human reason was intrinsically incapable of reaching

any certain knowledge about religious and moral issues. Thus, any apologetics was illegitimate. Theology's task was simply to preserve and proclaim the tradition.

The second method of refuting the rationalists was less radical. In it one attempted to adopt one of the prevailing contemporary philosophies to aid apologetics and systematic theology. There were several examples of such an approach, including the Tübingen school discussed above. Whereas the first approach was liable to an undue separation of the natural and supernatural realms, the usual charge against this second approach was an overidentification of these two realms.

The third approach saw itself as avoiding the dangers of the first two by working out a careful understanding of the relation of natural knowledge and supernatural revelation. To do this, it had to reject Enlightenment rationalism, which it accused of having lost touch with the true relation of faith and reason when it separated itself from the Catholic tradition. In place of Enlightenment rationalism, this approach recommended a return to the understanding of the relation of faith and reason found in Thomistic Scholasticism. As such, it was designated "neo-Scholasticism."

The determining characteristic of the period which spawned the interconfessional opposition over "fundamental theology" is that this earlier pluralism was forcibly replaced through the ecclesial endorsement of the third alternative as alone authoritative.[3] Negatively, between 1855 and 1866 both traditionalism and most of the "accommodation" approaches were explicitly condemned. This meant that almost every major force in Catholic theology except Scholasticism was removed from consideration as a legitimate alternative. Positively, with the publication of the Apostolic Constitution on Faith--*Dei Filius*--by the First Vatican Council in April 1870 and the release of the encyclical *Aeterni Patris* by Leo XIII in August 1879, Thomistic neo-Scholasticism was officially endorsed as the one true method of Catholic theology.[4]

The importance of this move for our consideration of fundamental theology cannot be overemphasized. We have seen that the earliest Catholic use of the term "fundamental theology"-- Ehrlich--preceded these events by ten years and was associated

with a work that was significantly divergent from the Scholastic
approach.[5] However, prior to Vatican I there were few, if any,
other explicit fundamental theologies published. By contrast,
between 1870 and 1900 there were at least twelve texts published
with this title. Significantly, all of these works utilized
a neo-Scholastic mode of apologetics that was devoid of the
phenomenological/hermeneutic emphases that had characterized
Ehrlich.[6] At first glance, this use of "fundamental theology"
to designate a neo-Scholastic approach rather than a self-
conscious alternative to such an approach is surprising. It
appears that the decisive stimulus for this switch came from a
key affirmation of Vatican I: "The correct use of reason
demonstrates the foundation (*fundamenta*) of faith" (DS 3019).
Indeed, this affirmation came to be known as "The Charter of
Fundamental Theology".[7] In this affirmation the Scholastic
preference for rational argumentation is closely conjoined with
the idea of providing a fundament for faith and theology. Thus,
the tendency for neo-Scholastic theologians to embrace the term
"fundamental theology" is not as astonishing as, at first sight,
it appears.

It was the neo-Scholastic conception of fundamental theology
that became the Catholic antipode in the interconfessional
opposition over fundamental theology. Accordingly, our next
task is to gain an understanding of this conception.

An understanding of the conception of the task and method
of fundamental theology inherent in the neo-Scholastic approach
can best be gained through an investigation of the question:
"What is the foundation of faith that the correct use of reason
demonstrates?" Such an investigation will reveal why this
approach became known as "objective apologetics."

It must first be noted that *Dei Filius* asserted that God
(and signs of divine revelation) "can be reliably recognized
in created things by the natural light of human reason" (DS 1785).
This recognition was understood to be grounded in a rigorous
rational demonstration.[8]

There is a crucial distinction, however, when we move from
knowledge of God's existence to knowledge of the *content* of
divine revelation. According to Vatican I, we cannot apprehend
by natural reason the truth of this content.[9] We apprehend

this truth through faith, not reason. Significantly, faith is
defined as a supernatural virtue "through which, motivated by
the grace of God, we believe that those things that God has
revealed are true . . . *on the basis of the authority of the
God who reveals*, and who can neither deceive nor be deceived"
(DS 3008, emphasis added). That is, we accept the Christian
revelation not because we apprehend the intrinsic truth of
what has been revealed but because we can be rationally convinced
that it has been endorsed with the authority of God. How are
we thus convinced?

> In order that . . . the obedience of our faith might correspond
> with reason, God desired to bind external proofs of God's reve-
> lation with the internal help of the Holy Spirit: i.e., divine
> works, above all miracles and prophecies. Since these amply
> demonstrate God's omnipotence and immeasurable knowledge, they
> are entirely certain and enable us to comprehend all appropriate
> signs of divine revelation (DS 3009).

In this sense, neo-Scholastic apologetics argued for the
rational appropriateness of the act of Christian faith on the
basis of the objective--i.e., available to natural reason
because grounded in external criteria--facts of miracles, pro-
phecy, and the existence of the Church. However, as McCool
warns, this apologetics did not try to rationally prove the
truth of the *content* of Christian faith; it merely tried to
show a rational and moral appropriateness for the *decision* for
Christian faith.[10] This distinction is often overlooked by
both Protestants and Catholics.

This separation of the *fact* of a divine revelation from the
content of that revelation dictated a very specific understanding
of the task and scope of fundamental theology. Totally unacceptable was an approach (like that of Schleiermacher or Drey)
that tried to ground Christian faith by explicating that faith
itself. Likewise, an approach which merely tried to ground
the traditional sources of theology was much too limited. The
only proper task of fundamental theology was to vindicate the
credibility of the existence of revelation and, given that
revelation, the moral necessity of the act of faith. As such,
fundamental theology dealt with the *praeambula fidei*.

One of the corollaries of this understanding of the task of
fundamental theology is that fundamental theology is radically
separated from dogmatics. For example, Joseph Kleutgen--the

most representative of the early neo-Thomist theologians--
explicitly asserts that fundamental theology and scientific
(i.e. doctrinal) theology are irreducibly distinct disciplines.[11]
We see here a regression from the closer affiliation of these
two disciplines that had been momentarily established with
Staudenmaier and Ehrlich.

While we will have occasion later to point out certain
limitations to this conception of fundamental theology, we
would note here two positive aspects inherent in it.[12] First,
neo-Scholastic fundamental theology saw its task as the media-
tion of faith to the world (even if its means for doing so
leave something to be desired[13]). Thus, it tried to develop a
dialogical method and structure--something emphasized in the
recent ecumenical discussion as desirable. Second, neo-
Scholastic fundamental theology began to formulate a concept
of theology as a science. That is, it incorporated questions
of theological method into its subject area. More exactly,
the "Roman" form of fundamental theology--as contrasted with
the "German" form[14]--included a theological *Prinzipienlehre*
within its boundaries.[15] However, as Stirnimann notes, this
development remained at a nascent stage, only achieving real
significance in the more recent discussion.[16]

B. *Protestant Developments: Karl Barth*

While Catholic theology was moving towards the affirmation
of the need and ability to show the rational credibility of
Christian faith, Protestants were moving in the opposite direction. For them, the stress was increasingly put on the unique
and essentially ungroundable character of Christian faith. Out
of faithfulness to this understanding of faith, they felt a
growing need to reject what they considered to be the "pagan"
approach endorsed at Vatican I and to avoid the term "fundamental
theology."[17] Epitomatic of this move was Karl Barth's dialectical
theology.

One of the best ways to approach Barth's strong anti-
apologetic formulations is to note a sympathetic interpretive
history of the development leading up to Barth's position. We
have in mind Werner Elert's *Der Kampf um das Christentum*,[18]
which is a summary of the Protestant understandings of apologetics

from the time of Schleiermacher on. A survey of the titles of
the various stages that Elert discerns in this discussion provides an insight into the direction of Protestant thought that
led to Barth.

At the beginning, with Schleiermacher, there was a period of
peaceful coexistence in which one can treat "Theology as a
Synthesis between Christianity and Science." In this setting,
as we have seen, Schleiermacher could construe apologetics as
grounding theology merely by expressing its essence.

This period of peaceful coexistence soon ended, however, with
the development of "A Separation of Christianity and Science"
inaugurated by the growing appropriation of the critical philosophy of Kant. Theology was isolated from philosophy and the
latter was de-Christianized. In this setting, apologetics
became "The Attempt to Restore the Synthesis." Importantly,
this restoration was attempted primarily in terms of a practical
defense of the legitimacy of religion and theology, not through
a reconsideration of such fundamental issues as the relation of
faith and reason.[19]

These practical attempts at restoration soon proved inadequate,
and attention was turned instead to the establishment of "The
Theological Autonomy of Christianity." As exemplified in Ritschl,
apologetics now turned to seeking out and emphasizing the uniqueness of Christianity.[20] Unlike Schleiermacher, this emphasis on
the nature of Christianity was not seen as an apologetics but
as proclamation.[21]

In line with this assertion of the autonomy of Christianity,
there arose the corollary of a "Culture without Christianity."
This situation sets the stage for the period immediately preceding
Barth. The disdain for this period can be seen in Elert's
designation of it as seeking "Synthesis out of Resignation." In
particular, he accuses these theologians of surrendering to the
attacks of non-Christian culture by using the standards of that
culture as a critical guide to restrict or reformulate their
theology. In his opinion, this move is a more blatant surrender
to culture than even the worst conservative apologetics that
preceded it.[22]

Elert does not end on this note of despair but rather with
a cry of welcome for the emerging "Renewal of the Christian

Awareness of Distance over-against General Culture" as signaled
in Kierkegaard. It is this new movement that Barth was to
appropriate and expand.

We must turn now to Barth himself. Our reason for focusing
on Barth is that he is the clearest, most polemical representative of the Protestant antipode in the interconfessional
opposition over the task and possibility of fundamental theology.[23]

In interest of historical accuracy, it must be admitted that
Barth was not always opposed to fundamental-theological concerns
and that he appears to have developed a chastened appreciation
of them in his later work.[24] However, his characteristic position in terms of the period of the debate now under consideration
is epitomized in his rejection of the approach of Vatican I as
being the work of the "Antichrist."[25]

The most immediate reason for this rejection is that Barth
discerns in this approach a presupposition that God is manifested in our creatureliness in such a way that God is directly
discernible by us.[26] For Barth, such an assumption threatens
the Reformation affirmation that all human knowledge and
experience of God is a gift of grace.[27] This is true even if
one argues that our knowledge of God is analogical, for Barth
insists that any possible analogy must lead from the Creator
to the creature, and not vice versa. It is an analogy that
exists if, and only if, God posits it in revealing activity.[28]
The approach of Vatican I appears, on the contrary, to assert
that, apart from the revelation of God in Christ, we humans
have the ability to gain rational conviction about the existence and nature of God. Such an approach seems to place the
human on the same level as God and fails to take sin seriously.[29]

The difference between Barth and neo-Scholasticism can be
illustrated from another direction by considering their treatment of the relation of faith and understanding. One of the
primary concerns of neo-Scholastic theology was to show that,
because of the credibility of the existence of revelation, the
decision of faith was rationally appropriate and morally necessary. In his book on Anselm, Barth establishes a quite
different approach by arguing that "the aim of theology cannot
be to lead men to faith, nor to confirm them in faith, nor
even to deliver their faith from doubt."[30] For Barth, knowledge

does not precede faith, but rather follows it. Knowledge is
not required to provide for the existence of faith, rather
faith's very nature provokes the desire for knowledge. It is
not a matter of faith requiring proof, but rather of faith
giving rise to the desire for understanding.[31]

It is important to note that behind this divergent understanding of the relation of faith and understanding lies an
essentially antipolar reaction of neo-Scholasticism and Barth
to the philosophical developments of the Enlightenment. The
essence of the Enlightenment philosophies was an inherently
critical attitude towards all external authority. As we have
seen, neo-Scholasticism rejected any such conception of the
relation of faith (or authority) and reason. Instead, it
called for a return to the approach of Aquinas (as the neo-
Scholastics understood Aquinas). Barth (and most Protestants),
on the other hand, tended to take the Enlightenment philosophies as legitimate dialogue partners for theology.[32] This
is not to say that they did not criticize these philosophies.
Indeed, Barth's approach to them was essentially to "stand
them on their head," i.e., to reverse the direction of thought
from "question--commitment" to "commitment--question." Nevertheless, it was the Enlightenment philosophies and not a
repristinated Thomism which focused the problems of Barth's
theological program. Since he was dealing with an understanding
of reason as inherently critical of all authority, it is no
surprise that he could see no role for reason in establishing
faith.

Barth's understanding of faith also entailed his understanding of the proper task of an apologetics. This task was *not*
to provide the ground or basis upon which faith can only sub-
sequently take place. Rather, it was to give "an account of
what happens *when* God is known."[33] That is, apologetics is
always a post-faith exposition of the one God in God's self-
revelation. This self-revelation is coextensive with the
revelation of the Word through the Holy Spirit. It can never
be separated in terms of a primordial "natural" revelation and
a later "christocentric" revelation. Thus, Barth rejected the
neo-Scholastic distinction between the content of faith, which

is not provable, and the existence of God or the divine signs
of revelation, which are.

An important implication of this understanding of the task
of apologetics is that it is necessarily very closely integrated
with dogmatics. Indeed, Barth argues that apologetics is only
possible if it is treated as a part of dogmatics.[34] His
criticism of most other conceptions of apologetics is precisely
that one has to set aside the dogmatic task to pursue the apologetic task.[35] This integration of apologetics and dogmatics,
along with its presupposition that fundamental-theological
reflection is a post-faith endeavor--i.e., the critical reflection of faith upon its own forms of expressions, etc., were to
be Barth's most important contributions to the subsequent
ecumenical discussion of fundamental theology.

There is one further point that is crucial to understanding
Barth's relationship to "fundamental theology." We have seen
that he did not use the term himself and that he radically
altered the understanding of apologetics that was usually
associated with the term. However, Barth did consider it
important to ground theology by reflecting on how theological
knowledge arises.[36] This was the task of his *Prolegomena to
Dogmatics*. As Joest points out, this was really a fundamental-
theological task, aimed at providing the basis for dogmatics.[37]

C. *Summary*

To summarize, the period currently under consideration witnessed the development of narrowed, antithetical positions on
both the Catholic and Protestant sides relating to the
possibility, task and method of fundamental theology. One of
the chief causes of this development was the Catholic identification of "fundamental theology" with a rationalistic
Scholastic apologetics. Most Protestants could not accept
such a discipline so they tended to reject "fundamental theology"
per se. However, they did preserve one significant task the
Catholic theologians were just beginning to assign to fundamental
theology--namely, the grounding of theology through a theological
Prinzipienlehre. In this sense, one could argue that Protestants
had not totally rejected fundamental theology; they had merely
reconceived it. Indeed, it has recently become common to

speak of a "Catholic" conception of fundamental theology which
is aimed at grounding faith and a "Protestant" conception which
is aimed at grounding theology.[38] Such a distinction does have
significant warrant in the time period we have just considered.
One of our questions in the next chapter is whether it remains
valid.

[1]See Wagner, "Fundamentaltheologie," p. 21. N.B., For purposes of
focus, we are limiting our consideration to the most polemical representatives of each tradition: neo-Scholasticism and Karl Barth. There were
alternative conceptions in each tradition, but their impact did not become
significant until the more recent discussion. Therefore, we will postpone
treatment of these alternatives until the next chapter.

[2]McCool, *Nineteenth Century*, pp. 18-19.

[3]A good summary of this reaction can be found in McCool, *Nineteenth
Century*, pp. 129-44.

[4]See McCool, *Nineteenth Century*, pp. 216-40, on the history and doctrine
of *Dei Filius* and *Aeterni Patris*. An English translation of *Aeterni Patris*
can be found in Jacques Maritain, *The Angelic Doctor* (NY: Dial Press,
1931), pp. 224-62.

[5]See Stirnimann, "Fundamentaltheologie," pp. 294-95fn1.

[6]Johannes Flury, *Um die Redlichkeit des Glaubens*, (Freiburg: Freiburg
Universität Verlag, 1979), p. 29.

[7]Wagner, "Fundamentaltheologie," p. 18.

[8]Henri Bouillard, "La Tâche actualle de la Theologie fondamentale,"
Le Point Theologique 2 (1972): 18.

[9]More precisely, while reason might be able to know a few of the truths
revealed by God, it cannot know them all (DS 3005, 3015).

[10]McCool, *Nineteenth Century*, p. 178. To properly appreciate *Dei
Filius* it is necessary to note that it was directed *against* a rationalism
that tried to demonstrate the intrinsic rationality of the content of faith.
Cf. Bernard Lonergan, *Method in Theology*, (NY: Seabury, 1972), p. 320.

[11]Ibid.

[12]Suggested by Flury, *Redlichkeit*, pp. 84-85.

[13]Cf. Metz, *Faith*, p. 18.

[14]On the difference between these two forms see Schmitz, "Fundamentaltheologie," p. 199.

[15]Flury, *Redlichkeit*, p. 59. The "German" form of fundamental theology
assigned method questions to dogmatics rather than fundamental theology.

[16]Stirnimann, "Fundamentaltheologie," p. 329.

[17]It would be an interesting study to determine the last early Protestant use of this term. In light of their reticence regarding the term, our

study of the Protestant understanding of fundamental theology during this
period must center on the cognate concerns of apologetics and questions
of theological method.

[18] (Munich: Beck, 1921).

[19] Ibid., p. 215.

[20] Ibid., p. 258.

[21] See Ritschl's disavowal of any apologetic interest as cited in Ebeling,
"Fundamentaltheologie," p. 497fn39.

[22] Elert, *Der Kampf*, p. 367.

[23] The more moderate dialectical theologians will be treated in the
following chapter--to the degree that they initiated the move away from
Barth's polemical position and towards a more fruitful interconfessional
dialogue.

[24] A good treatment of the developments in Barth's attitude towards
these concerns can be found in: Attila Szekeres,"Karl Barth und die
natürliche Theologie," EvTh 4 (1964): 229-42.

[25] Barth, *Church Dogmatics*, I.1: x.

[26] Ibid, p. 130.

[27] Ibid., II.1: 74.

[28] Ibid., p. 83.

[29] Ibid.

[30] Karl Barth, *Anselm. Fides Quarens Intellectum*, (London: SCM,
1960), p. 17.

[31] Ibid., pp. 18, 16.

[32] Wolfhart Pannenberg, *The Idea of God and Human Freedom*, (Phil.:
Westminster, 1973), p. 117.

[33] Barth, *Church Dogmatics*, II.1: 8; emphasis added.

[34] Ibid., I.1: 45.

[35] See, for example, his critique of Brunner's "eristics" in Ibid., 29.

[36] E.g., Barth, *Church Dogmatics*, I.1: 25, 43.

[37] Joest, *Fundamentaltheologie*, p. 9.

[38] E.g., Heinrich Petri, "Die Entdeckung der Fundamentaltheologie in der
evangelischen Theologie," *Catholica* 33 (1979): 245.

CHAPTER THREE
INTERCONFESSIONAL DIALOGUE ABOUT
FUNDAMENTAL THEOLOGY

Based on our exposition of the most polemical representatives
in the interconfessional opposition over fundamental theology
one might easily despair over any possibility of an interconfessional rapprochment concerning this topic. And yet, this
is precisely what is taking place. To properly understand this
surprising development we must first consider the changes that
made such a rapprochment possible.

A. *Developments Towards Interconfessional Dialogue*

As mentioned earlier, the two extreme antipodes in the interconfessional opposition over fundamental theology were not
without their critics, even at the beginning. Especially as
these positions reached a stage of development where their
implications and limitations became more evident, critical
voices and alternative conceptions began to be advanced within
the individual confessions themselves. The long-term result
of this was twofold. First, some of the extreme points of the
dominant positions were modified or eliminated. Second, and
just as important, the legitimacy and fruitfulness of approach-
ing fundamental-theological questions from a plurality of
viewpoints was once again accepted on both sides.

In this section we will note some of the most significant
of these developments, which were to provide the basis for the
explicit discussion of an ecumenical fundamental theology. For
purposes of continuity, we will treat first the Catholic developments and then the Protestant. However, the mutual influence
of the two should not be overlooked.

1. Catholic Developments

We will treat the developments in the Catholic reconsideration of fundamental theology at some length, due both to their
significance in preparing the way for the present dialogue and
to the relative lack of acquaintance with these developments in
Protestant circles.[1] It should be noted that the first two
movements treated in this section significantly predate our
current temporal focus. However, the real impact of these
early critiques was only felt in the period now under consideration so their treatment here is justified.[2]

a. *Immanence Apologetics*. The most significant of the
earlier rivals of the neo-Scholastic understanding of apologetics
is associated with the work of Maurice Blondel[3] and has come
to be known as "immanence apologetics."[4] Blondel's approach
developed as a critique of the rationalism and extrinsicality
of neo-Scholastic apologetics. In his first major work--*L'Action*
(1893), his doctoral dissertation--Blondel undertook to develop
a philosophical approach to meaning in human life that was not
limited merely to that which is rationally knowable. He chose
human action as a comprehensive category that integrated
reason, will and emotions and sought to show how reflection on
human action could be an organon for truth. Our actions incar-
nate our grasp of reality and offer us the possibility of
knowing it conceptually. Thus, living is prior to philoso-
phizing. This means that the only proper apologetic is one
that reflects *post factum* on an actual faith commitment. Such
a reflection shows that this commitment is always a response
to a call for faith presented by tradition and the Christian
community. Thus, the ultimate goal of a proper apologetic is
to justify the openness to this call of faith and/or to try
to awaken a readiness to respond to that call.[5] This justification would not proceed by arguing rationally that divine
revelation is possible and has in fact taken place. Blondel
doubted that such an extrinsic approach could ever create an
obligation for us to believe. Instead, he sought to demonstrate
phenomenologically that the inner structures of human action
necessarily bring an individual to a "threshold" where they are

challenged to believe, and thus enter true life; or refuse faith, and thus go counter to their destiny.[6] Blondel maintained that this option, while offered to all human beings, is most fully and concretely presented in the life, death and resurrection of Jesus Christ. Thus, his was an apologetics for Christian faith based on the inner dynamic of human life, rather than external arguments about the authority of the revealing God.

Two notes are in order about this approach of an immanence apologetics. First, Blondel himself never called for an ultimate choice between his apologetics and traditional apologetics. Rather, he saw the two as complementary.[7] Second, even though Blondel's approach was essentially rejected as being modernist,[8] it continued to exercise significant influence in writings on pastoral apologetics through the first half of the twentieth century. By contrast, it was seldom defended as a scientific apologetic until the post-Vatican II theological discussion.[9]

b. *Internal Neo-Scholastic Critique.* As the exclusion of the alternatives to neo-Scholasticism became more complete, the only signs of theological life to be found in the Catholic Church were those within neo-Scholasticism itself. Thus, any alternative conceptions had to be presented as critical reflections on the scholastic heritage in light of criticisms such as Blondel's. The main focus of these reflections was on determining the real motives of faith and the role of faith in constructing a fundamental theology.[10] The most fruitful period of such critical reflections within neo-Scholasticism was the first ten years between the wars. From 1925 onwards there was a very noticeable regression as the Church became more and more preoccupied with purely ecclesiastical matters.[11]

Among the most significant contributions to this critical reflection was the work of the Jesuit Pierre Rousselot. Rousselot's essential project was the attempt to show that the approach to apologetics developed by Blondel was not antithetical to "authentic" Thomism. In his dissertation *The Intellectualism of St. Thomas,*[12] he challenged the "philosophical excommunication" of Blondel by showing that the rationalistic conceptualism of the neo-Scholastic manuals was not entirely appropriate to Thomas himself. Rather, he argued

that Thomas' real position was able to overcome the seeming
contradiction between the deductive neo-Scholastic approach
and Blondel's reflection on the act of faith. In his famous
article "Les Yeux de la foi,"[13] he went even further in investigating the relationship between the act of faith and the
knowledge of credibility. In this study he arrived at the
conclusion that the credibility of Christian revelation can
only be recognized by the eyes of faith (hence the title).
The act of faith and the act of recognizing credibility are
one and the same. Rousselot concluded the article by then
trying to justify this approach as true to Thomas by appealing
to Thomas' understanding of love as the basis of real knowledge.

Obviously, such an understanding of the relation of faith
and the knowledge of credibility had significant implications
for the understanding of theology as a whole and fundamental
theology in particular. Most significantly, it made fundamental
theology truly theological by stressing that it starts from
revelation and faith.[14] Thus, the neo-Scholastic separation
between fundamental theology and dogmatics is implicitly
rejected.

These implications for fundamental theology were soon ex-
plicated by two other important theologians. The Dominican
Ambrose Gardeil commented at length in *Le donné révélé et la
théologie* (1910) on the implications of this rediscovery of
the light of faith. He concluded that if faith is not merely
a neutral acceptance of the truths of revelation, but rather
the inward recognition of that truth, then theology is no
longer a neutral science that can be practiced without faith.[15]
Likewise, the Tübingen theologian Karl Adam inferred from the
stress on the identity of the recognition of credibility and
the act of faith that the only true "way of theology" was a
thinking that starts with faith and proceeds by faith.[16]

These various attempts at criticizing or reformulating a
neo-Scholastic apologetics were summarized in a suggestive
fashion by Karl Eschweiler who argued that in the time between
the wars there were essentially two "ways of theology."[17] The
first of these was the way of apologetic confrontation; the
second, that of dogmatic self-reflection. Essentially, the first
was that of neo-Scholasticism (which Eschweiler, to the chagrin

of the neo-Scholastics, compared to the semi-rationalism of
Günther) while the second reflected the impact of the work of
Rousselot *et al*. Eschweiler himself defends the second position,
thus criticizing the neo-Scholastic separation of fundamental-
theological reflection and dogmatic reflection. It is important
to note, however, that Eschweiler does not reject apologetics.
Rather, he reformulates its task as being the reflection of
theology on itself--i.e., a theological *Prinzipienlehre*.[18] The
similarity of this conception to that which Barth was just
beginning to develop is striking. Unfortunately, immediately
following the publication of Eschweiler's book, the conservative
regression of Catholic theology referred to above set in and
most of the contributions of the theologians just summarized
were lost to the interconfessional discussion of the time.

c. *Stimuli towards Vatican II*. It was over twenty-five
years before significant criticism of the dominant neo-Scholastic
approach to apologetics could again surface. Significantly, a
primary cause of this reappearance was renewed acquaintance with
the criticisms of the previous generation and (later) a rediscovery of the pluralistic roots of the discipline in the
nineteenth century. This time the criticism could not be
stifled. Instead, it became an important stimulus for the
Catholic Church's renewed reflection on the nature of faith at
Vatican II.

At first; the renewed criticism of neo-Scholastic apologetics
concentrated on specific problems of that approach. For example,
Gottlieb Söhngen gave a detailed critique of the traditional use
of miracles as a rational grounding of faith by arguing that
this use went contrary to the Bible's own understanding of the
nature and purpose of miracles.[19]

An even more significant development was the publication in
1953 by Albert Lang of the first full fundamental theology
based on the new understanding of faith derived from Blondel
and Rousselot.[20] It is characteristic that, as opposed to
traditional apologetics which tried to demonstrate the *reasonable* and *necessary* nature of the will to believe on the basis
of the *external criteria* of revelation, Lang saw his new
apologetics as "placing special value on awakening the

readiness for faith of modern persons by displaying the value
of faith and seeking to present it as the fulfillment of the
inclinations and needs of essential human nature."[21] This
demonstration of the value of faith was conducted through a
presentation of the contents of faith.[22] Thus, here again we
see the apologetic and dogmatic tasks closely conjoined.

It is particularly significant for our investigation that
Lang departed from the neo-Scholastic practice of using "fundamental theology" and "apologetics" interchangeably. He
defended the preference of the former over the latter on the
grounds that "apologetics" emphasizes the negative task of
defending the faith against attacks while "fundamental theology"
carries a more positive connotation.[23]

Lang's book proved to be truly ground-breaking. It was not,
however, without its limitations. In particular, it continued
to operate with a simplistic view of history inherited from
the old apologetics. It also retained what must be considered
a rationalistic tone.[24] Perhaps this helps explain why it was
not given any notice by Protestant literature during its first
ten years of publication.[25]

Another important stimulus towards Vatican II was the intense
creative work in patristic, liturgical, and above all biblical
theology following W.W. II. This work had been spawned at the
encouragement of Pope Pius XII and soon led to important revisions of the theological understanding of revelation, tradition
and the nature of faith.[26] These revised understandings
presented a pressing demand for correlated revisions in the
understanding of fundamental theology.

One final important stimulus was the rediscovery of the
Catholic Tübingen school. It will be recalled that, in the
latter half of the nineteenth century, Catholic theology, under
the influence of neo-Scholasticism, had pushed the Tübingen
school to the periphery of theological thought. This meant
that the concerns of dialogue with modern thought and contemporary Protestant theology which these theologians had
epitomized were temporarily stifled. However, just prior to
Vatican II, there was a rediscovery of the nature and importance of this school and its promise for contemporary
theological discussion.[27] As Metz points out, the rehabilitation

of the Tübingen school meant implicitly a reaffirmation of
their concern for dialogue with modern philosophical and
Protestant thought.[28]

   d. *The Impact of Vatican II*. The combined impact of these
various influences significantly shaped the final formulations
of Vatican II. In turn, the documents of Vatican II became
a springboard for the intense creative work in fundamental
theology that characterizes the present debate. It is thus not
inappropriate that the constitution *Dei Verbum* came to be known
as the "charter" of the new fundamental theology.[29]

   Rather than attempting to summarize all of Vatican II's
teachings on faith, revelation, etc., the most convenient way
to show its significance for the changing Catholic understanding
of fundamental theology is to consider a significant collection
of essays dealing specifically with this question. This collection was published in 1969 as volume forty-six of the
Concilium series under the title *The Development of Fundamental
Theology*.[30] It is, without a doubt, the best introduction to
the recent discussion of fundamental theology in Catholic circles. It comprises a collection of essays dealing with the
shortcomings of the old style of fundamental theology and
suggesting some tentative new directions. It does not claim to
provide a consensus on what a new fundamental theology should
be, only some significant aspects that it must incorporate.
We will briefly summarize the most important of these.

   The central change in the approach to fundamental theology
signaled by Vatican II is a renewed appreciation of the inherent
certainty of faith. As Walgrave puts it: "It is now stressed
that as an existential event faith contains all it needs for
its own certainty."[31] With this change, it is no longer considered to be the task of fundamental theology to provide a
prior "objective" basis for the act of faith. Rather, its
task is to explicate the certainty inherent in faith itself.

   A direct implication of the previous point is that the neo-
Scholastic understanding of a strong separation between
fundamental theology and dogmatics is rejected. As Segundo
points out, this neo-Scholastic approach assumed a human possibility of declaring Christianity to be true before knowing

what it said. This is evident when they tried to conduct their
discussion with nonbelievers in terms of the *praeambula fidei*.
By contrast, Vatican II totally reversed this approach by
declaring explicitly that dialogue with nonbelievers is realized
with what properly constitutes dogmatic theology.[32] Thus, the
fundamental-theological and dogmatic tasks are integrally
connected.

If this is true, then the only possible method for finding
the foundations of faith and theology is a posteriori.[33] The
implication of this is that fundamental theology stands at the
end of theological reflection, not at its beginning. This
implication will affect not only how fundamental theology is
constructed but how it is taught.

Another characteristic of the new fundamental theology is
a deeper appreciation of the constructive role of dialogue
with nonbelievers. The old style apologetics had tended to
regard the truth it was defending as an unassailable fortress
which was to be preserved intact at all costs. Thus, its
major concern was to rebut error. By contrast, the main concern of the new fundamental theology is to create a basis for
dialogue.[34] This new concern spawned the realization that
this dialogue may well lead to reformulations of the theological affirmations under discussion. It is precisely this new
understanding of the main concern of apologetics that leads
these authors to endorse Lang's preference for the designation
"fundamental theology" over "apologetics."[35]

One final important characteristic of Vatican II pertaining
to fundamental theology is that it endorsed the biblical subordination of any experience of God through the created world
to the experience of God's revealing activity in history.[36]
This was a direct implication of the closer association of
fundamental theology with the dogmatic exposition of biblical
faith. Its results can be found in the unique *heilsgeschichte*
approach to fundamental theology developed in *Mysterium Salutis*--
the five-volume outline of dogmatics developed in conjunction
with Vatican II.

e. *A Renewed Pluralism*. This brings us to the last significant development in the Catholic approach to theology that

prepared the ground for the present ecumenical dialogue--namely, the reemergence of an accepted pluralism of methods for Catholic theology.[37] We will briefly note a few of the alternative approaches that found currency in the early post-Vatican II Church.

First, the growing critical movements within neo-Thomist circles gave birth to a distinct alternative even under the banner of Thomism. Of course, there continued to be a few works written in essentially the classic neo-Scholastic manner. Much more common, however, have been works drawing on the "transcendental" reading of Thomas worked out by Rahner and Lonergan.[38]

The alternatives go beyond those that explicitly designate themselves as Thomist. As just mentioned, an approach which stressed the "saving history" of the biblical materials was developed in *Mysterium Salutis*. The basic assumption of this approach is that theology is more profitably pursued along the lines of concrete saving history than according to abstract metaphysical principles (like Thomism).[39] Likewise, it assumed that confrontation with biblical revelation is primary and that fundamental-theological reflection is necessarily subsequent. The purpose of this reflection is 1) to show the openness of the human for receiving this *heilsgeschichte*, 2) to work out the fundamental structures and concepts of this *heilsgeschichte*, and 3) to mediate the responsible confrontation of these categories with modern thought.[40]

A rather unique alternative which blended many aspects of the *heilsgeschichte* approach with the basic approach of Albert Lang was worked out by Adolf Kolping.[41] Characteristic of Kolping is the conviction that the essential task of fundamental theology is to give a rational grounding of the act of faith by seeking to awaken a willingness and inclination towards the obedience of faith (I:26). What is crucial to note in this definition is that he restricts fundamental theology to grounding faith as opposed to grounding the science of theology (I:76). For him, the task of grounding theology is an abstract, speculative task for theology as a whole, not fundamental theology in particular (I:35-36).

Kolping's very stress on the distinction between grounding faith and grounding theology shows that his opinion was not

universally held. Indeed, there was another approach to fundamental theology that strongly stressed its role of grounding
theology--i.e., of being a theological *Prinzipienlehre*. Characteristic of this approach is Gottlieb Söhngen.[42] What is
particularly important about the work of Söhngen and others like
him is that we see here, for the first time in a "German"
fundamental theology, the inclusion of a theological *Prinzipienlehre* as part of the task of fundamental theology.[43] Metz
sees this as the most significant of the recent developments
because it signals a general consensus among Catholic theologians on the necessary correlation of grounding faith and
grounding theology.[44]

   While this list is not exhaustive, it does serve to illustrate
the point that the post-Vatican II discussion of fundamental
theology has been characterized by a renewed awareness of the
benefit and/or necessity of tolerating a plurality of distinct
approaches.

2. Protestant Developments

   The developments in the Protestant discussion that prepared
the way for the present ecumenical dialogue can be more rapidly
summarized. In the words of Schubert Ogden: "The safest
generalization about Protestant theology since W.W. II is that
it has evidenced a growing concern with its inescapable apologetic
task."[45] Obviously, this growing apologetic concern had to
confront Barth's strong disparagement of such a concern. It
did so primarily by arguing that Barth had not really overcome
the problems that called for an apologetics but rather had
simply "pushed them under the carpet."[46] It then proceeded to
defend the apologetic task by arguing that such a task was an
irrelinquishable life-expression of the Christian Church and
a necessary element of all Christian theology.[47]

   Even more devastating to Barth's attempt to remove the
apologetic concern from Protestant theology was the emerging
realization of an underlying apologetic in Barth himself.
Pannenberg has convincingly argued that Barth's very rejection
of natural theology functioned itself as an apologetic against
the atheistic critiques of the metaphysical idea of God.[48]
Along the same line, Birkner has argued that the *function* of

a natural theology is not absent from Barth's theology; it is
merely replaced by Feuerbach's critique of religion. That is,
the latter shows the place and meaning (albeit negative) of
all talk of God.[49]

It is also important to note that while Barth was a significant theological voice in the period following W.W. II, he
hardly commanded total assent--even among dialectical theologians! As early as 1929 Emil Brunner had defended "the
other task of theology"--i.e., apologetics.[50] This difference
in perspective grew into an open split with the publication
of an article on natural theology that provoked a firey "No!"
from Barth.[51] The tenor of recent Protestant theology has
reflected an inclination towards Brunner's position in this
debate, as opposed to Barth.

It is commonly recognized that the other dialectical theologians also reveal, in practice, powerful apologetic
tendencies.[52] Tillich is particularly noteworthy because he
explicitly developed this apologetic concern into a theory of
correlation.[53] It was his opinion that the kerygmatic
theologians--preeminently Barth--could only achieve true theological validity if they too took this method of correlation
seriously.[54] The significance of this is that post-war
Protestant theology, both in America and in Europe, has
increasingly leaned toward Tillich's appreciation of apologetics,
while the influence of Barth has waned.[55]

This shift in the appraisal of apologetics was correlated
with a shift in the understanding of the relation of faith and
reason. Essentially, this new understanding has aimed at a
renewed appreciation of reason within its proper role. Inherent
in this new understanding is a critique of the stance that Barth
took to the Enlightenment philosophies. In practice, Barth had
accepted the Enlightenment claim of the radical autonomy of
reason and then tried to "trump" this atheistic reason with a
radical belief in revelation. Pannenberg is representative of
the new understanding when he characterizes this move by Barth
as "an excessive adaptation of theology to the intellectual
fashions of the age."[56] By contrast, the move endorsed by the
new discussion is towards an understanding of the role of
reason as based on faith and explicating faith with an eye

towards those outside of faith. As Macquarrie argues, under
such a conception faith would not be rationally grounded, but
it would be tested in the light of all the knowledge and experience we have at our disposal.[57] It is precisely in light of
this new understanding of the relation of faith and reason that
Gilkey can argue for the legitimacy of apologetics--understood
as the attempt to show the relevance and meaning (and even in
some cases the validity) of the Christian view of things--
while rejecting the pursuit of natural theology--understood
as the attempt to demonstrate the validity of certain doctrines
of faith *solely* on the grounds of general experience and
rational argumentation, without explicit appeal to any revel-
ational authority.[58] That is, the new understanding of
apologetics focuses on its hermeneutical function of showing
the meaning of Christian faith rather than its traditional
function of objectively demonstrating truth.

3. The Setting of the Interconfessional Dialogue

Further insight into the development towards interconfessional dialogue over fundamental theology can be obtained by
noting a change in the "setting" of fundamental-theological
reflection which helped prepare for this dialogue. It will be
recalled that fundamental theology arose in response to the
challenge of the Enlightenment. Moreover, we saw that a basic
difference in the manner of response to this challenge lay
behind the stark antipodes of the period of interconfessional
opposition. It is thus of great significance that the growing
rejection of the traditional opposition over fundamental
theology has been characterized as a direct result of an
"enlightenment about the Enlightenment."[59] That is, contemporary theologians have realized that both a total rejection of
Enlightenment philosophies (neo-Scholasticism) and an excessive
adaptation to them (Barth) are ultimately unprofitable stances.
Instead, drawing on recent philosophical, psychological and
sociological critiques of Enlightenment thought, these
theologians have sought to come to terms with the "New Water-
shed in Theology" caused by the "ending of the Enlightenment."[60]

Of primary importance to our investigation is the fact that
the interconfessional response to this new "setting" of

fundamental-theological reflection has been much more unified
than the response to the original Enlightenment. For example,
Catholics have explicitly drawn on Protestant resources in
framing their response.[61] It is our contention that this convergence in the manner of response to the contemporary
post-Enlightenment philosophies (e.g., Marxism, Heremeneutic
Philosophy, Structuralism, etc.) is the underlying basis for
the convergence in conceptions of the task and scope of fundamental theology. This can best be seen by considering some of
the characteristic emphases of the post-Enlightenment philosophies.

One of the most significant of these characteristics is the
surrender of the ideal of a single perennial philosophical
system. Instead of emphasis on the construction of such a
perennial system, there has developed a critical awareness of
the plurality of philosophical approaches and an emphasis on
philosophy as critical maieutic reflection rather than metaphysical construction.[62] This has been directly reflected in
fundamental-theological discussion by the realization that
there is no single Protestant or Catholic philosophy and thus
that a plurality of approaches must be tolerated--with particular emphasis placed on the hermeneutic and critical
approaches.[63]

An immediate corollary of the reconception of philosophy as
a critical and hermeneutic enterprise is that questions of
method have become central, for the question of the truth of
an assertion is now framed in terms of *how* one formulated the
assertion and how one could test it. This has been paralleled
in contemporary theology--both Protestant and Catholic--by a
marked increase in concern for method.[64] This move is very
significant for our discussion, for it helps to illustrate our
contention that the inclusion of questions of theological
method in a discipline treating the question of the truth of
Christian faith was a necessary move that reflected the contemporary philosophical setting of the discipline.[65]

Another significant characteristic of many post-Enlightenment
philosophies is the rejection of the Enlightenment "prejudice
against preunderstanding."[66] That is, there is a renewed
appreciation for the role that commitment and tradition play

in the understanding process. This renewed appreciation has
contributed significantly to the development, in both confessions, of a more adequate conception of the relation of faith
(tradition, authority, etc.) and reason. This new conception
strives to preserve the insights of Blondel, Rousselot, Barth,
et al. pertaining to the constitutive role of belief in knowing,
without unduly deprecating the role of reason in providing
faith with self-awareness. As noted above, one of the important
implications of this new understanding has been an overcoming
of the separation of fundamental theology and dogmatics. This
is an ecumenically significant development because--as Pesch
notes--the separation of these two was significantly motivated
by the Reformation.[67] The overcoming of this separation would
thus appear to be a necessary step in ecumenical rapprochment.

4. Summary

In brief, the various developments we have been considering
served to lessen the differences between the two confessions
regarding fundamental theology. We noted that one of the ways
to describe the interconfessional opposition over fundamental
theology was to say that Catholics focus the discipline on
grounding faith while Protestants focus it on grounding theology.
In the period now under consideration the warrant for this
characterization was significantly diminished. On the one hand,
questions of theological method were accepted within the scope
of fundamental theology by a growing number of Catholic theologians.[68] On the other hand, there was a widespread
reacceptance of the legitimacy of the task of grounding faith
among Protestants.

To be sure, there remained differences between the two
confessions regarding these matters. A basic difference in
their conception of how best to ground faith provides a good
example. Kolping suggestively pictures this difference as the
fact that Protestants seek merely to remove hindrances to the
leap of faith while Catholics go further in trying to create a
basis for this leap.[69] The important thing to note is that this
is no longer a difference concerning the legitimacy of the task
of grounding faith. Rather, it is a difference regarding questions of the goal and method of a mutually accepted task;

differences that may well be moderated by explicit dialogue
between the confessions.[70]

It is easy to see how the various developments we have
treated led away from the interconfessional opposition over
fundamental theology and towards explicit interconfessional
dialogue. We must turn now to an account of that dialogue and
its results.

B. *Explicit Interconfessional Dialogue*[71]

The beginnings of the explicit interconfessional dialogue
over fundamental theology are associated with the Protestant
theologian Gerhard Ebeling.[72] In 1968 he assumed the Chair of
Fundamental Theology and Hermeneutic at Zürich--the first such
Protestant chair and one created especially for him. A year
later he published the second volume of his collected essays
with the subtitle "Beiträge zur Fundamentaltheologie und zur
Lehre von Gott."[73] Then, in 1970, he published the article
"Erwägungen zu einer evangelischen Fundamentaltheologie." As
noted earlier, a central aim of this article was to awaken an
historical consciousness of the Protestant precedents for a
fundamental theology. However, it also developed some preliminary characteristics of a contemporary Protestant fundamental
theology--partly through dialogue with Catholic fundamental
theologians. These preliminary suggestions were more fully
developed by Ebeling in his later writings.[74]

Early initiative in developing this dialogue was evident
on the Catholic side as well. As post-Vatican II fundamental
theologians strove to fulfill their mandate to come to terms
with modern thought, they found significant help in the work
of Protestant thinkers who had preceded them in this task. For
example, when Schillebeeckx tried to come to terms with the
fundamental-theological issue of hermeneutics, he found more
help from Protestants like Bultmann and Gadamer than from
contemporary Catholic theologians.[75]

From these rather limited beginnings, the dialogue has
slowly spread on both Protestant and Catholic soil.

The development has taken three forms on the Protestant
side. First, a growing number of Protestant theologians have
begun to use the term "fundamental theology" as a designation

for certain of their theological activities. For example, in
1971 Pannenberg asserted that theological anthropology was a
type of fundamental theology.[76] By 1973 he was also using
this term to designate a foundational discipline that provided
a phenomenological location of Christianity within the world
religions.[77] In 1974 Gerhard Sauter began to correlate a
"meta-theory of theology" with fundamental theology.[78] By
1975 the movement had "crossed the sea," and we find such
American theologians as Edward Farley, Langdon Gilkey and
Peter Hodgson using the term to designate a fundamental ontology
of human existence.[79]

A second form this development has taken among Protestants
is the production of a full-fledged Protestant fundamental
theology. Actually, there is to date only one such work:
Wilfried Joest's *Fundamentaltheologie. Theologische Grundlagen
und Methodenprobleme*.[80] However, Horst Beintker has produced
an outline of another such program.[81]

The third--most direct--form the developing dialogue has
taken is the explicit consideration of the history of Catholic
fundamental theology as a means of developing criteria for a
Protestant fundamental theology. Unfortunately, this form has
not found many representatives. The only significant work is
the praiseworthy contribution of Johannes Flury.[82]

On the Catholic side the explicit dialogue has likewise
taken three forms. First, there have been several significant
reviews of the various Protestant contributions.[83] These
reviews have endeavored both to learn from the Protestant
discussion and to critique its shortcomings.

A second form the Catholic discussion has taken is the
historical investigation of the early interconfessional origins
of fundamental theology.[84] This investigation has produced
an awareness of early Protestant examples of fundamental theology. More importantly, it has shown that there is warrant in
the Catholic tradition itself for distinguishing between
fundamental theology per se and its neo-Scholastic exemplification. Such warrant lends support to the contemporary
endeavors to reformulate fundamental theology in an ecumenical
direction.

Finally there has been the production by Peter Knauer of a
full-scale fundamental theology that explicitly aimed at being
ecumenical and that entered into extensive dialogue with Protestant fundamental theologians--especially Ebeling.[85]   An outline
of a similar work has been produced by Stirnimann.[86]

C. *Results of the Interconfessional Dialogue*

Our account of the explicit interconfessional dialogue over
fundamental theology should have made it clear that this dialogue
is spreading and has reached a level that warrants the serious
attention of theologians. What is not yet clear are the results
of this dialogue. What progress has been made in the development of *an* ecumenical fundamental theology?

The first thing we should note is that the warrant for
making a strong distinction between the "Catholic" conception
of fundamental theology as aimed at grounding faith and the
"Protestant" conception of fundamental theology as aimed at
grounding theology has been further diminished. On the one
hand, there has been an even closer approximation of the Protestant and Catholic understandings of the relation of faith
and reason. We had noticed a continuing basic difference just
prior to the explicit dialogue. However, as the dialogue spread,
theologians on both sides attempted to integrate the value of
the alternative approach into a dialectical interpretation
that preserves the value of both.[87] The result is that the
difference between the two confessions in this regard could
recently be judged as "hardly of great significance."[88] On the
other hand, the acceptance of questions of theological method
into the scope of fundamental theology by Catholic theologians
has continued to spread.[89]

Thus, whereas it was once felt that there was one Catholic
mode of fundamental-theological reflection and a totally different Protestant mode, we can now find Protestant and Catholic
representatives for each of the several different approaches.[90]
Indeed, it is not uncommon now to find intraconfessional
disputes over the task and scope of fundamental theology given
more consideration than the interconfessional disputes.[91]

One must not infer from these developments, however, that
a unanimous acceptance of a particular conception of the task,

scope and method of an ecumenical fundamental theology has
emerged. Rather, the interconfessional discussion has been
populated by several distinct conceptions of the task and scope
of the discipline. In light of the fact that a central characteristic of the setting for the interconfessional dialogue is
the acceptance of a plurality of approaches, such diversity
seems unavoidable. The best that can be hoped for is a consensus over the essential task of a fundamental theology and
the interrelationship of the various approaches in helping to
fulfill this task. However, to date, even this level of
consensus is lacking.

In brief, the interconfessional split over the possibility
of a fundamental theology has been bridged. However, a general
interconfessional consensus on the basic task, scope and
method(s) of an ecumenical fundamental theology has not yet
been achieved. A significant obstacle to such a consensus is
that there has not been a detailed typological comparison of the
various proposed understandings of this discipline that have
populated the recent discussion. Such a comparison would
show similarities and differences, expose overlaps, and suggest
means of cooperation between the various approaches. As such,
it is indispensable to the continuing progress of the discussion
of an ecumenical fundamental theology.

The development of such a typology is the task to which we
now turn.

---

[1] The significant exception to this judgment is Johannes Flury, who has
pursued an in-depth study of these developments. See especially *Um die
Redlichkeit des Glaubens*.

[2] Note, for example, that Rousselot's "Les Yeux de la Foi" (1910) was
not translated into German--and thereby made central to the discussion--
until 1963.

[3] See especially: *The Letter on Apologetics, and History and Dogma*, (NY:
Holt, Rinehart & Winston, 1965). The best English secondary summaries of
Blondel are Gregory Baum, *Man Becoming*, (NY: Herder, 1970), pp. 1-36;
Henri Bouillard, *The Logic of Faith*, (NY: Sheed & Ward, 1967), pp. 161-85;
and Bernard Reardon, *Liberalism and Tradition*, (Cambridge: Cambridge
University Press, 1975), pp. 222-42.

[4]The definitive history of this approach is E. Seiterich, *Wege der Glaubensbegründung nach der sogennanten Immanenzapologetik*, (Freiburg: Herder, 1938).

[5]Schmitz, "Fundamentaltheologie," p. 220.

[6]Baum, *Man Becoming*, p. 19.

[7]Schmitz, "Fundamentaltheologie," pp. 206-7.

[8]Although Blondel was not personally condemned due to his irenic nature, his basic approach was generally considered modernist at heart. Cf. Reardon, *Liberalism*, pp. 241-42.

[9]As late as 1959 it could be argued that the traditional neo-Scholastic apologetics was the only scientific apologetics. E.g., N. Dunas, "Les problèmes et la statut de l'apologétique," RSPhTh 43 (1959): 659-60. More recently, Blondel's approach has been reaffirmed and developed by theologians such as Baum, Bouillard and Rahner.

[10]Thus, it is no accident that the definitive secondary treatment of these developments—by Roger Aubert—is titled *Le Probléme de l'acte de foi*, (Louvain: Warney, 1950). This work gives excellent treatments of Rousselot, Gardeil and Adam.

[11]T. Mark Schoof, *A Survey of Catholic Theology—1800-1970*, (NY: Paulist and Newman Press, 1970), p. 87.

[12](London: Sheed and Ward, 1935).

[13]RSR 1 (1910): 241-59, 444-75.

[14]Adolf Kolping, *Fundamentaltheologie*, 3 vol. (Münster: Regensberg, 1968-1981), I: 23.

[15]Schoof, *Catholic Theology*, p. 190.

[16]Flury, *Redlichkeit*, p. 149. See especially Adam's *Glaube und die Glaubewissenschaften*, (Rottenburgln, 1923).

[17]*Die zwei Wege der neueren Theologie*, (Augsburg, 1926).

[18]Ibid., pp. 245-47.

[19]Gottlieb Söhngen, "Wunderzeichen und Glaube. Biblische Grundlegung der katholischen Apologetik," in *Die Einheit in der Theologie*, (Munich: K. Zink, 1952), pp. 265-85.

[20]Albert Lang, *Fundamentaltheologie. Bd. I, Die Sendung Christi* (1953); *Bd. II, Der Auftrag der Kirche* (1962), (Munich: Max Hueber).

[21]Ibid., I: 22.

[22]Ibid., I: 28.

[23]Ibid., I: 44. Note, however, that he also argues that both tasks must be incorporated in an "integral apologetics." Ibid., I: 33. Cf. Kolping, *Fundamentaltheologie*, I: 25; and Heinrich Fries, "Eine neue Fundamentaltheologie," ThQ 134 (1954): 460fn1.

[24]Cf. Gößmann, "Fundamentaltheologie," p. 40fn29.

[25]A fact noted by Adolf Kolping, "Zehn Jahre einer neuen Fundamental-theologie," MThZ 15 (1964): 62-69.

[26]Cf. Schoof, *Catholic Theology*, pp. 210-11.

[27]See especially Joseph Geiselmann, *Die katholische Tübinger Schule*, (Freiburg: Herder, 1964).

[28]Metz, *Faith*, p. 22.

[29]Bouillard, "La Tâche," p. 20. The neo-Scholastics had used this designation for the Vatican I constitution *Dei Filius*.

[30]Ed. J. B. Metz, (NY: Seabury, 1969).

[31]Jan Walgrave, "The Essence of Modern Fundamental Theology," *Concilium* 46 (1969): 82.

[32]Juan Segundo, "Fundamental Theology and Dialogue," *Concilium* 46 (1969): 71, 73.

[33]Raymond Pannikkar, "Metatheology or Diacritical Theology as Fundamental Theology," *Concilium* 46 (1969): 47.

[34]Cf. Heinrich Fries, "From Apologetics to Fundamental Theology," *Concilium* 46 (1969): 58.

[35]Ibid., pp. 57-59.

[36]Gerald O'Collins, *Fundamental Theology*, (NY: Paulist Press, 1981), pp. 72-73.

[37]See McCool, *Nineteenth Century*, pp. 241-67, where he specifically cites (263) a basic alternative between a radically altered Thomistic theological method (Rahner, Lonergan) and an evolved and radically altered Tübingen theological method (Kasper). These alternatives, while significant, are not exclusive.

[38]A good example of the latter type is O'Collins, *Fundamental Theology*.

[39]Eduard Schillebeeckx, *Revelation and Theology*, (London: Sheed and Ward, 1967), II: 86.

[40]Adolf Darlap, "Fundamentaltheologie des Heilsgeschichte," in *Mysterium Salutis*, (Einsiedeln: Benziger, 1965), I: 14-15. On this approach in general see Eduard Stakemeier, "Zur heilsgeschichtlichen Orientierung der Fundamentaltheologie nach dem Zweiten Vatikanum," *Catholica* 21 (1967): 101-126.

[41]*Fundamentaltheologie. Bd. I, Theorie der Glaubwürdigkeitserkenntnis der Offenbarung* (1968); *Bd. II, Die konkretgeschichtliche Offenbarung Gottes* (1974); *Bd. III, Die katholische Kirche als die Sachwalterin der Offenbarung Gottes. I. Teil: Die geschichtlichen Anfänge der Kirche Christi* (1981), (Münster: Regensberg).

[42]"Fundamentaltheologie," LThK[2] IV, 452-59.

[43]The "Latin" fundamental theologies had always contained this concern--see above, p. 31.

[44]Metz, *Faith*, p. 23.

[45]Schubert Ogden, *The Reality of God*, (NY: Harper & Row, 1963), p. 120.

[46]Joest, *Fundamentaltheologie*, p. 41.

[47]E.g., Kurt Aland, *Apologie der Apologetik*, (Berlin: Walter de Gruyter, 1948), p. 17.

[48]Pannenberg, *Idea of God*, p. 100.

[49]H. J. Birkner, "Natürliche Theologie und Offenbarungstheologie," NZSTh 3 (1961): 294.

[50]Emil Brunner, "Die andere Aufgabe der Theologie," ZZ 7 (1929): 255-76.

[51]The two articles--"Nature and Grace" by Brunner and "No!" by Barth--
are collected in *Natural Theology*, (London: Centenary Press, 1946).

[52]Langdon Gilkey, "Trends in Protestant Apologetics," *Concilium* 46
(1969): 130-31.

[53]Paul Tillich, *Systematic Theology*, (Chicago: University of Chicago
Press, 1951), I: 8.

[54]Ibid., p. 7. In Gilkey's opinion, the rest of the dialectical theologians did in fact follow this method, even though they rejected it in
theory. Gilkey, "Trends," p. 137.

[55]Cf. Heinz Zahrnt, *The Question of God*, (NY: Harcourt, Brace &
World, 1969), p. 295; and Ogden, *The Reality of God*, p. 5.

[56]Pannenberg, *Idea of God*, p. 87.

[57]John Macquarrie, "The Problem of Natural Theology," in *Thinking
About God*, (NY: Harper & Row, 1975), p. 135.

[58]Gilkey, "Trends," pp. 130-31.

[59]Heinrich Petri, "Fundamentaltheologie im Umbau," ThGl 69 (1979): 95.

[60]See the essay by this name in Langdon Gilkey, *Society and the Sacred*,
(NY: Crossroad, 1981), pp. 3-14. See also Geffré, "Recent Developments,"
p. 12.

[61]See, for example, Monden's appeal to Protestant theology for help in
confronting the problem of historicity. Monden, *Faith*, p. 6.

[62]See the Forward to Paul Ricoeur, *Main Trends in Philosophy*, (NY:
Holmes & Meier, 1979), wherein he distinguishes five basic trends of modern
philosophy, only one of which consciously aims at constructing an embracive
Weltanschaung--and even this one is acutely aware of the limits of such an
enterprise.

[63]See H. Beintker, "Verstehen und Glauben, " KuD 22 (1976): 38; and
J. B. Metz, "Apologetics," EnTh, pp. 22-23.

[64]Cf. John Cobb, *Living Options in Protestant Theology*, (Phil.: Westminster, 1962), p. 9; and McCool, *Nineteenth Century*, p. 6.

[65]We see this suggestion as much more convincing than that of Flury who
viewed the turn from concern for grounding faith to concern for grounding
theology as simply a result of the fact that modern educated persons were
ignoring fundamental theology. Flury, "Fundamentaltheologie," pp. 358-59.

[66]See Hans-Georg Gadamer, *Truth and Method*, (NY: Seabury, 1975), esp.
p. 239.

[67]Otto Pesch, "Fundamentaltheologie und Dogmatik. Erwägungen zu einer
unvermeidlichen aber problematischen Unterscheidung," in *Unterwegs zur
Einheit*, eds. J. Brantschen & P. Selvatico (Freiburg: Herder, 1980), p. 452.

[68]Cf., above, p. 48.

[69]Kolping, *Fundamentaltheologie*, I: 67.

[70]Cf. Gilkey, "Trends," pp. 128-29.

[71]It is not our aim here to summarize the various understandings of
fundamental theology represented in the present interconfessional dialogue.
That is the task of the typology in part two. Presently, we are concerned
with a brief account of the history of the developing dialogue.

[72]The first contemporary Protestant work to designate its project as "fundamental theology" was actually Ray Hart's *Unfinished Man and the Imagination*, (NY: Seabury, 1968), p. 14. However, Hart explicitly mentions his indebtedness on many counts to his study under Ebeling (p. 177fn110), and the use of this terminology is probably one of them.

[73]*Wort und Glaube, II*, (Tübingen: J.C.B. Mohr, 1969). Note also pp. iv, 104.

[74]See especially *Introduction to a Theological Theory of Language*, (Phil.: Fortress, 1973)--note p. 181; and *The Study of Theology*, (Phil.: Fortress, 1978), esp. pp. 153-65.

[75]Eduard Schillebeeckx, "Towards a Catholic Use of Hermeneutics," in *God the Future of Man*, (NY: Sheed & Ward, 1968), pp. 3-49.

[76]Pannenberg, *Idea of God*, p. 90.

[77]Pannenberg, *Theology and Philosophy of Science*, p. 417.

[78]Sauter, *Grundlagen*, p. 67.

[79]Edward Farley, *Ecclesial Man*, (Phil.: Fortress, 1975), p. 72; Langdon Gilkey, *Reaping the Whirlwind*, (NY: Seabury, 1976), p. 369fn3; Peter Hodgson, *New Birth of Freedom*, (Phil.: Fortress, 1976), p. 114.

[80](Stuttgart: Kohlhammer, 1974).

[81]"Verstehen und Glauben," KuD 22 (1976): 22-40.

[82]"Was ist Fundamentaltheologie?" ThZ 31 (1975): 351-67; and *Um die Redlichkeit des Glaubens*, (Freiburg: Freiburg Universität Verlag, 1979).

[83]See especially Seckler, "Evangelische Fundamentaltheologie"; Heinrich Stirnimann, "Evangelische Fundamentaltheologie," FZPhTh 22 (1975): 375-83; and Petri, "Die Entdeckung der Fundamentaltheologie in der evangelischen Theologie."

[84]The best examples are Wagner, "Fundamentaltheologie"; and Stirnimann, "Erwägungen zur Fundamentaltheologie."

[85]Peter Knauer, *Der Glaube kommt vom Hören: Ökumenische Fundamentaltheologie*, (Cologne: Styria, 1977).

[86]"Erwägungen zur Fundamentaltheologie."

[87]E.g., Gilkey, *Society and the Sacred*, p. 36.

[88]Pesch, "Fundamentaltheologie," p. 455.

[89]E.g., Stirnimann, "Erwägungen zur Fundamentaltheologie," pp. 329-32.

[90]It will be part of the task of the typology in part two of this project to establish this point by illustrating each position with both Protestant and Catholic sources, wherever possible.

[91]For example, Peter Knauer, in a review of W. Joest's *Fundamentaltheologie* (ThPh 51 {1976}: 607-9), spent more time defending Joest's understanding of the task of fundamental theology against its Catholic critics (esp. Seckler) than he did critiquing the book itself.

PART TWO

CONTEMPORARY UNDERSTANDINGS OF
FUNDAMENTAL THEOLOGY

INTRODUCTION

The second major task of this essay is to present a typological description of the contemporary interconfessional
discussion of fundamental theology. There are two characteristics of this typology that must be noted at the outset.

First, it will focus on the *task*, *scope* and *method* of
fundamental theology. Individual theologians' answers to
particular fundamental-theological problems will be considered
only insofar as they contribute to this focus.

Second, this typology will be structured as an outline of
the various elements ascribed to the task of fundamental theology. It will not give a sequential treatment of the individual
theologians. The latter approach was rejected due to two
characteristics of the way in which theologians treat fundamental-theological matters. First, it is quite common for a
theologian to treat these matters under several different
headings. For example, Rahner uses at least five such headings[1]
while a summary of Ebeling's fundamental theology must deal
with at least four.[2] Second, careful investigation often shows
that a particular theologian can incorporate two or more
quite distinct tasks under the single heading of fundamental
theology.[3] While these practices may not be illegitimate, they
do make simple summaries of individual positions difficult,
both to construct and to compare.

For these reasons we will structure the typology in terms
of the various elements ascribed to the task of fundamental
theology. Individual theologians will be treated in correlation with the particular elements they discuss. Obviously, this
approach does not completely solve the problems just mentioned,
for it will often be necessary to treat theologians in relation
to more than one element. Thereby, we are surrendering the
(desirable) attempt to provide readily accessible summaries
of the individual theologians.[4] However, the advantages

gained by our approach justify this concession. In particular, this approach will demonstrate an interconfessional representation for each of the major aspects--thereby substantiating our claim of a "working" ecumenical consensus regarding the task and scope of fundamental theology.[5]

The typology, then, is structured around the various elements ascribed to the task of fundamental theology. What are these elements? They can be organized around two major poles. One pole conceives the major task of fundamental theology to be the grounding of the Christian faith. The other centers this task in the grounding of Christian theology (as the self-reflective activity of the Christian community). The first alternative focuses on showing that the commitment to Christian faith is appropriate and, indeed, desirable. The second focuses on providing the critical methodological basis for the various theological enterprises.

An understanding of the difference between these two alternatives can be gained by considering how each would deal with conversion. The first approach sees conversion as its goal--i.e., all fundamental-theological reflection aims at justifying and facilitating conversion.[6] The second approach, by contrast, sees conversion (or the givenness of the Christian "fact") as its starting point--i.e., that from which it must develop the basis for theology as self-reflection.[7] This illustration is particularly helpful because it not only shows the distinctiveness of each emphasis, it also suggests their connection; namely, the first approach grounds that upon which theology is based while the second focuses on rendering this foundation accessible to theology.

Our typology, then, will be presented in two major divisions: "Fundamental Theology as Grounding Faith" (chapter four) and "Fundamental Theology as Grounding Theology" (chapter five). Within each of these major divisions we will survey the various elements of fundamental theology's overarching task.

Following the typology proper, we will devote special consideration to the question of "The Place of Praxis in Fundamental Theology" (chapter six). This isolation of the issue of praxis was deemed the most helpful way of assessing the legitimacy and contribution of the recent attempts to develop political

theology as a fundamental theology.   This is not a third set
of elements involved in the task of fundamental theology but
rather a concentration on the place of praxis within the two
sets previously summarized.

[1]These include traditional fundamental theologie (*Fundamentaltheologie*),
apologetics, the new fundamental theology (*fundamentale Theologie*), formal
and fundamental theology, and his so-called Foundational Course.

[2]Ebeling conducts fundamental-theological investigations under the
titles: "The Evidentness of the Ethical," "Hermeneutic Theology,"
"Theological Theory of Language" and "Theological Encyclopedia."

[3]For example, David Tracy appears to use "fundamental theology" as a
designation for two significantly different tasks: first, a reflection on
the method and criteria of theological argument (*Blessed Rage for Order*,
{NY: Seabury, 1973}, p. 15fn8); second, an academically oriented argument
for the basic logically ordered questions of religion, God and Christ
("Defending the Public Character of Theology," *Christian Century* 98
{1981}:   352).

[4]Note, however, that an approximation to such summaries can be obtained
through use of the index of principal names at the end of this essay.

[5]Of particular importance in this regard is that, while some have
argued that the conception of fundamental theology as aimed at grounding
faith is a "Catholic" approach and the conception of fundamental theology
as aimed at grounding theology is "Protestant," we will show Catholic and
Protestant representatives for both these major emphases. Cf. Petri,
"Entdeckung," p. 245.

[6]E.g., Lang, *Fundamentaltheologie*, I: 22-29; and Seckler, "Evangelische
Fundamentaltheologie," p. 290.

[7]The best example is Lonergan, who sees foundational theology as "an
objectification of conversion (which) provides theology with its foundations"
(*Method in Theology*, {NY: Seabury, 1972}, p. 130). As Tracy correctly
notes, Lonergan's foundational theology does not try to justify critically
the act of conversion, rather it assumes conversion as a given and seeks to
show how objectification of this "given" provides the basis needed for the
theological enterprises of doctrine, systematics and communications
("Lonergan's Foundational Theology. An Interpretation and Critique," in
Foundations of Theology, ed. Philip McShane {University of Notre Dame Press,
1971}, pp. 197-222, esp. 210).

CHAPTER FOUR
FUNDAMENTAL THEOLOGY AS
GROUNDING FAITH

The first major grouping of elements in a fundamental theology focuses on the task of grounding Christian faith. While some
representatives frame this concern in terms of addressing nonbelievers with the intent of facilitating their conversion,[1]
the primary thrust is increasingly focused on providing post
facto explication of the various grounds and motives involved
in an existing faith commitment.[2]

We will organize the various elements of this overarching
task by adapting the three-step outline of classical Christian
apologetics: *demonstratio religiosa*, *demonstratio christiana* and
demonstratio ecclesiastica. Accordingly, the first section of
this chapter will focus on formulations of fundamental theology
that emphasize the task of demonstrating the presence of a
dimension of ultimacy or the "religious"[3] in human existence.
The second section will be devoted to the role of the presentation of the specifically Christian message in grounding faith.
The third section will focus on the unique place that consideration of the Christian community can play in this task.

Our adaptation of this outline from classical apologetics
should not be misconstrued as implying that the task of grounding
faith is entirely synonymous with apologetics. The term
"apologetics" is usually understood to connote the defense of
the faith in view of the objections of nonbelievers. As we
noted above, the fundamental-theological concern to ground
faith is equally involved in facilitating a self-understanding
of faith among believers. More importantly, apologetics traditionally tried to justify faith with philosophical and
historical arguments that did not presuppose a knowledge of
the contents of Christian faith. The majority of the positions
treated in this chapter consider such an approach both

impossible and unrewarding. Instead, they ground faith precisely
from the viewpoint of the meaningfulness and value of this content.[4] Rather than assuming that the subject of this chapter
is necessarily apologetics, one of our concerns will be to
differentiate between apologetic and nonapologetic formulations
of the various elements.[5]

Support for our point that fundamental theology's task of
grounding faith is not synonymous with apologetics can be
found in the final two sections of this chapter. An increasing
number of fundamental theologians are asserting that the various positions treated in our first three sections--which at
least approximate the apologetic concern--are not capable of
adequately or effectively grounding faith. In place of these
positions (or alongside them), these theologians call for a
significantly different manner of grounding faith. These
alternative approaches fall into two groups. First, there are
those who stress the need to reflect psychologically, socio-
logically, as well as theologically on the act of conversion
itself in order to adduce from it the character and motives of
conversion. Second, there is the unique approach, initiated
by Karl Rahner, of a foundational course (*Grundkurs*) as a
prelude to theology proper.

A. *Demonstratio Religiosa*

Under this heading most neo-Scholastic fundamental theologies
undertook to demonstrate the universal human need for a supernatural revelation and the universal capacity to receive such
a revelation. However, this is no longer the way this task
is construed. As Bouillard points out, the earlier approach
was framed in a setting where the main dialogue partners of
Christian fundamental theology were deists and adherents of
other faiths. Thus, it was not the existence of God that was
in most question but rather the need for a special revelation
from God and the legitimacy of the Christian claim to be that
revelation. Contemporary fundamental theology finds itself in
a radically new situation. It faces not deists or religionists
but atheists. As such, its main problem is not the doctrine of
revelation but the doctrine of God.[6] Accordingly, the primary
task focused by the heading *demonstratio religiosa* is the

demonstration of the validity and meaning of "God" or, as a
modest prelude to that task, the demonstration of a "religious"
dimension in human existence.

Our analysis of a *demonstratio religiosa* will be divided into
three parts. First, we will consider those formulations of
this task which concentrate on a demonstration of the presence
of a "religious" dimension in human existence. Second, we will
deal with those formulations which stress the necessity of
moving beyond this mere demonstration towards the construction
of an ontology or a metaphysical view of reality inclusive of
this dimension. Finally, we will consider a significant alternative to the first two approaches which engages in a type of
negative *demonstratio religiosa*. That is, it seeks to uncover
not the existence of a positive "religious" dimension in human
existence but rather a negative "point of contact" at which
the transcendental reality and/or call of God can become
effective.

1. A "Religious" Dimension in Human Existence

The first set of emphases in a *demonstratio religiosa* limits
its task to the demonstration of a "religious" dimension in
human existence. Representatives of this approach have construed
the procedure for such a demonstration in at least three different ways: a) through a phenomenological analysis of human
existence, b) through conversation with the human sciences, and
c) through linguistic analysis.

a. *Phenomenological Analysis of General Human Existence.*
One of the most concise definitions of fundamental theology from
this perspective is that of Peter Hodgson who sees it as "A
phenomenological description of basic structures of the human
being's experienced existence in the world, which may provide
. . . a foundation for the experience of revelation and language
about God."[7] As he goes on to say, this approach does not
present a deductive argument for God, rather it merely describes
human existence as it is. It does not *prove* but rather *lets us
see* the situation in which revelation is a possibility.

One of the best examples of this approach in action is
Langdon Gilkey's *Naming the Whirlwind*.[8] In this work Gilkey

develops a "prolegomenon to Christian theology" whose task is
"a discussion of the possibility of God-language in a secular
time through a demonstration of its usefulness or meaningfulness,
in fact, its necessity for the ordinary life of man"(232). The
emphasis on the "ordinary" aspects of human life is characteristic of Gilkey's approach. He assumes only the character of
secular life, not the existential reality of faith (233). Thus,
his attempt to uncover the *meaning* of the religious symbol
"God" is not conducted through reflection on the religious
uses of this term but rather by examining our actual existence
in the world and trying to uncover there a hidden or forgotten
dimension of ultimacy (243).[9] The uncovering of this dimension
functions as a *demonstratio religiosa* in two ways. First, it
demonstrates the existence of a religious dimension precisely
in secular experience where it is most contested. Second, it
provides a basis for showing the "secular" meaningfulness of
explicitly religious language.[10] As such, Gilkey's prolegomenon
has an apologetic thrust, but it is an apologetic of *meaning*,
not validity;[11] or, to put it in other words, it discloses
fundamental convictions, it does not establish them (441).

A Catholic example of this approach can be found in chapter
five of David Tracy's *Blessed Rage for Order* where he seeks to
show "The Religious Dimension of Common Human Experience and
Language" through a phenomenological analysis.[12]

b. *Conversation with the Human Sciences*. Wolfhart Pannenberg's earliest usage of the term "fundamental theology" referred
to a theological anthropology.[13] He understood this anthropology
to be constructed through consideration of the various fields of
anthropological study (psychology, sociology, history, etc.),
their methods, results and problems, and the history of the
problems resulting from philosophical reflection upon human
subjectivity. The particular focus of these considerations is
on their implications for the religious dimension of human existence (93). The goal of such a theological anthropology would be
a demonstration of the religious dimension of human existence
(94), primarily by arguing that such a dimension is necessary
to do justice to the human openness to the world that the anthropological sciences have demonstrated.[14]

c. *Linguistic Analysis.* A unique approach to the provision of a *demonstratio religiosa* has been developed by Gerhard Ebeling in terms of a theological theory of language.[15] Ebeling characterizes his project as fundamental-theological in nature (187). Its primary task is to reflect on the mutual relationship of the language of general human experience and that of theology (182). Obviously, this is a reformulation of the question of the relation of general human experience and "religious" experience in light of the "linguistic turn" of contemporary philosophy.

Ebeling's central claim is that it is precisely the consideration of the nature of language in general that leads to an understanding of what "God" means.[16] The decisive function and power of language is to make present what is not immediately obvious (53). As such, the word "God" represents the extreme and most pure possibility of language, for "in it language affirms the presence of what is completely hidden" (55). If this is true, then the only way to have a comprehensive theory of human linguisticality--which Ebeling considers the essence of the human (98)--is to admit the legitimacy of "God-talk" and develop a theological theory of language (185). The implication is that a comprehensive view of the human must include, and indeed be grounded in, a dimension corresponding to religious language.[17]

2. A Metaphysics which Includes the "Religious" Dimension

So far we have considered those approaches which limit the *demonstratio religiosa* to establishing a dimension of ultimacy in human existence. We turn now to a second group of formulations which stress the need for a *demonstratio religiosa* to move beyond mere description and engage in a metaphysical (or ontological) grounding of this description.[18] The advocates of the need to develop such a grounding can be divided into two major groups: First, those who focus on developing an appropriate concept of God (a); and second, those who confine themselves to developing an anthropology (b).

a. *Focus on "God".* One of the strongest advocates of the need for fundamental theology to develop a metaphysical

conception of God is David Tracy. Tracy's approach includes
many similarities to Gilkey's attempt to establish phenomenologically a "religious" dimension in human existence. However,
while Gilkey limits his concern to this basic task and is very
suspicious of metaphysical categories,[19] it is characteristic
of Tracy's approach that he stresses the need to move beyond
the phenomenological portrayal to a transcendental reflection
that is charged with vindicating the presuppositions uncovered
in such a phenomenology as meaningful *and* true.[20]

In light of this need for a second stage of reflection,
Tracy devotes chapters in his fundamental theology to a defense
of the use of metaphysical categories in dealing with God and
to a tentative utilization of Process metaphysics as the most
defensible formulation of God-language and its meaning.[21]

A Protestant example of this approach can be found in Schubert
Ogden's defense of philosophical theology.[22] Ogden understands
the task of philosophical theology to be metaphysical in
nature: namely, to understand our common faith as an answer
to the basic question of the reality of God (65). Since the
question of God is by its very nature metaphysical, it can only
be adequately answered metaphysically by showing transcendent-
ally that God either is or is not the inclusive object of all
our faith and understanding (69). Thus, the main task of
philosophical theology is the metaphysical examination of the
notion of God (71).[23]

Such a forthright defense of metaphysics is surprising in
light of the reticence to use such language that we noted as
characterizing the new setting of fundamental-theological
reflection in part one of this essay. These theologians are
not, however, unaware of the limits of their enterprise.
Indeed, Tracy rejects the idea that he is bringing religion
before the judgment seat of metaphysics. Rather than such a
"hard" line of metaphysical reasoning, he sees his approach as
making the "soft" claim that the disclosure of a "limit-of"
dimension in human existence implies a "limit-to" as the
Ground of this dimension.[24] Thus, these theologians are
defending a chastened view of metaphysics.

b. *Focus on Anthropology*. Tracy's reference to the relation
of a "limit-of" dimension of human existence to a "limit-to"
Reality provides a helpful transition to the other major approach
to transcendental (in this case, ontological[25]) reflection as
part of a *demonstratio religiosa*. Representatives of this type
are reluctant to make statements about the nature of God. Nonetheless, they find it necessary to deal with the human as one
who is God-oriented. Thus, they focus their attention on the
construction of an anthropology.

This emphasis on anthropology has taken both an apologetic
and a nonapologetic form. The apologetic form seeks to demonstrate a type of "religious apriori" as constituent of human
existence. By contrast, the nonapologetic version takes the
believing person as a "given" and strives for a descriptive
ontology of such a person.

1) Demonstrating a Religious Apriori. Karl Rahner's
Hearers of the Word[26] is an example of this approach. Rahner
understands this book to be a treatment of an aspect of traditional fundamental theology (*Fundamentaltheologie*) which is
usually neglected (22). As such, it partakes in the general
fundamental-theological task of providing a rational foundation
for faith (17). Rahner's special concern within this larger
task is to develop an ontology of the *potentia Oboedientialis*
for revelation (3). That is, he seeks to illumine the apriori
human capacity for receiving revelation and, moreover, to show
that this revelation is not already an integral part of human
nature (19). His goal is to justify a conception of the human
as one who listens in his or her history for a possible revelation from God (22). In his later works, Rahner admits the
similarities of this conception to that of a "religious apriori"
but prefers to call it a "supernatural existential." Thereby,
he hopes to convey his contention that this capacity is constituent of human being while still affirming it is a gift of
grace.[27]

The Protestant Edward Farley inherited from Catholic theology
a similar understanding of fundamental theology. He defines it
as a "fundamental ontology which explores the *transcendental*
foundations of the possibility of faith."[28] He explicitly
correlates this with a demonstration of a religious apriori.

Such a demonstration is aimed at showing that human beings are
so constituted that knowledge of God is essential and proper
to them (130) or, conversely, that redemption and revelation
correspond to what is essentially human (131).[29]

2) Construction of an Ontology of Revelation. The second
group of theologians concerned with ontology are not so much
interested in arguing that we need revelation as they are in
simply asking what must be true about human existence in light
of the fact that revelation and faith do exist. For example,
Gerald O'Collins shows more reserve than his mentor Rahner when
he distinguishes between apologetics and fundamental theology,
limiting the task of the latter to 1) reflecting on the source
of (given) theological knowledge, and 2) calling attention to
the way human experience is open to receive that revelation.[30]

An intriguing, if occasionally opaque, presentation of this
approach by a Protestant can be found in Ray Hart.[31] For Hart,
fundamental theology has no apologetic interest (14,21). Rather,
it assumes revelation as a given fundament of human being (72)
and seeks to explicate this fundament through a regional ontology and a phenomenology of linguisticality (92). That is, it
ponders what must be true of human beings such that revelation
can be inserted into our being (120). The key results of this
reflection are an emphasis on the unfinished (i.e., emergent)
nature of human being (167) and on the role that imagination
plays as a goad to the human striving for completion (181-82).
Thus, Hart's basic task is to provide an ontological foundation
for the "religious" dimension of human existence through an
analysis of the imagination.[32]

3. Description of *Negative* Point of Contact for the "Religious"

The third type of *demonstratio religiosa* considers itself a
significant alternative to the first two approaches. It rejects
the attempt to prove the existence of a positive "religious"
dimension in human existence. Instead, it focuses on locating
a negative "point of contact" in human existence where the
transcendental reality or call of God can become effective.
Gerhard Ebeling is an important representative of this approach.

Ebeling's emphasis on the hermeneutical character of theology
is well-known. Integral to this emphasis is his assertion that

theology can accomplish its task of giving an account for
faith only if it acknowledges that it is grounded in a tradition
which precedes it, not some type of *praeambula fidei*.[33]   Likewise, the only adequate and effective ground of faith is the
human encounter with the Word-Event of tradition as re-presented
in contemporary proclamation.

Given this emphasis, one would expect Ebeling to be very
critical of the type of endeavor we have designated *demonstratio
religiosa*.   Indeed, if this endeavor is construed as providing
a *positive* basis upon which the subsequent decision for faith
can transpire, then Ebeling does reject it.[34]   However, there
is evident in Ebeling's fundamental-theological reflections a
recurring reference to a type of negative *demonstratio
religiosa*.[35]

An example of this move can be found in his reflections on
the meaning of "God."[36]   For Ebeling tradition is the key
source from which we must derive our understanding of God (336).
However, it is irrational to imagine that in speaking of God
we are completely at the mercy of tradition.   A purely traditional relation to God would be only a special kind of
godlessness for one would not adequately recognize what tradition means by "God."   Thus, we must seek a direct knowledge or
a personal experience which can be correlated with tradition
(339).   Ebeling locates this experience of what the word "God"
means within the sphere of the radical questionableness of
human existence.   This experience is not a positive consciousness of God.   It is only the condition on which such
consciousness of God could arise (347).[37]

Thus, Ebeling's *demonstratio religiosa* aims not at manifest-
ing a hidden positive "religious" dimension in human existence
but rather at making evident the questionableness of human
existence which is the condition for understanding and receiving
the message of tradition.   This negative approach is most
fully developed in his attempt to base theology on an "evidentness of the ethical."[38]   This essay is devoted to a
phenomenological analysis of the ethical dimension of human
existence.   It seeks to reveal several self-evident "compulsions",
the last of which is the compulsion to render account--an
ethical expression of the questionableness of human existence

(117-21, 123-25). The importance of this analysis is that it
describes the situation within which the word "God" finds its
meaning--as the answer to the question of human existence (124).
Such an investigation is fundamental in the sense that it sup-
plies the presupposition for actual theology--i.e., theology
can fulfill its task of answering for faith in Christ only by
answering for the radical questionableness uncovered in such
an investigation.[39]

A Catholic representative of such a negative *demonstratio
religiosa* is Henri Bouillard.[40] Bouillard sees the task of
fundamental theology as the investigation of the correspondence between the Christian message and human reality (24-25).[41]
This correspondence is shown by demonstrating that the Christian
message gives a response to the radical question implied by
human existence (33). The first step of a fundamental theology
is a presentation of this question. The point of departure for
such a presentation is found within contemporary ethical philosophy (36). One must seek within the radical problems of
secular ethical reflection those which correspond to the
Christian message of salvation (37).

There is an obvious affinity between Bouillard's position
and that of Ebeling. However, Bouillard gives an implicit
criticism of the extreme nature of Ebeling's distinction
between the question of human existence and the answer of
revelation--and thereby points to a closer relationship between
the negative *demonstratio religiosa* and the positive--when he
asserts that the passage from the question to the answer is
only possible if the question already anticipates the response
by delineating its contours. The divine answer to the question
of human existence would never be recognized if it did not
present itself in a form which was anticipated by the question
(39). Accordingly, a complete *demonstratio religiosa* must not
only explicate the questionableness of human existence--and
thus our openness to revelation--it must also reflect on the
type of response which is anticipated in and by this openness.

B. *Demonstratio Christiana*

Some fundamental theologians consider the task of grounding
faith as complete in the *demonstratio religiosa*. For example,
Ebeling moves directly from his demonstration of the self-
evident questionableness of human existence to the task of
theology proper, which is to account for Christian faith in
such a way that it also accounts for this radical questionableness.[42] Similarly, Gilkey restricts his prolegomenon to
establishing the meaningfulness of religious discourse in
general as a preparation for Christian theological discourse.[43]
He carefully distinguishes such a prolegomenon from theology
proper, which makes an assumption about the truth and meaningfulness of a particular (Christian) interpretation of the
general religious dimension disclosed by the prolegomenon. The
prolegomenon itself cannot deal with the validity of such a
particular interpretation.[44]

Most fundamental theologians, however, see the transition
from a general *demonstratio religiosa* to a particular *demonstratio christiana* as a necessary and appropriate one.[45]
There are even some who consider a *demonstratio christiana* as
the proper starting point for a fundamental theology which is
concerned to ground faith. For these theologians, the *demonstratio religiosa* is either self-evident--and therefore,
unnecessary--or an illegitimate attempt to ground Christian
faith in an extra-Christian reality.

We will discuss the various formulations of a *demonstratio
christiana* in terms of two basic methods employed in such a
demonstration: either 1) a correlation of Christian revelation
and general human experience, or 2) a comparative religions
analysis of Christianity's claim to validity.

1. Correlation of Revelation and General Human Experience

The most common type of *demonstratio christiana* attempts a
correlation of general human experience and Christian revelation. Depending on the particular theologian, the purpose of
this correlation can range from merely showing the meaning of
the claims of Christian revelation to the more apologetically
conceived goal of demonstrating the *appropriateness* and/or

truth of these claims. The most significant disagreement among representatives of this approach, however, is not the choice between an apologetic or nonapologetic correlation but rather the question of what direction any correlation should move-- i.e., does it move a) from general human experience to Christian revelation, or b) from Christian revelation to general human experience?

a. *General Human Experience - Christian Revelation.* The basic movement of a correlation from general human experience to Christian revelation will take on variations in accordance with whether one focuses on 1) positive human experience, 2) negative human experience, or 3) the ambiguous conjunction of these two.

1) Positive Human Experience. One of the clearest examples of a *demonstratio christiana* that starts with positive general human experience and moves to Christian revelation is the approach of David Tracy.[46] Tracy proposes a model for a revisionist theology whose main task is a correlation of com- mon human experience and language with the essential Christian tradition as revealed in an historical and hermeneutical investigation of classical Christian texts. The truth of the results of this correlation is then considered through a transcendental reflection (43-52).

We have already noted Tracy's arguments for the "religious" dimension of human experience and the necessary metaphysical grounding of this dimension. Our interest here is in his treatment of the uniquely Christian claims in a fundamental theology.

Tracy's *demonstratio christiana* begins with a chapter on "Religious Language in the New Testament"(119-45). He had previously developed an understanding of limit-language as demonstrative of the "religious" dimension in human existence. In this chapter he proceeds to show that the religious language of the New Testament is just such limit-language and thereby corresponds to common human experience (e.g., 109).

In his chapter devoted to christology (204-36) he focuses the *demonstratio christiana* more sharply to argue that 1) christological language is also a limit-language; 2) the

meanings of this language include the same cognitive claims
as the religious theism defended in his *demonstratio religiosa*;
and 3) christological language is existentially meaningful
(224fn9).

The most important point, for our purposes, about Tracy's
formulation of a *demonstratio christiana* is that he explicitly
works *from* human experience *to* Christian revelation. This is
best seen in his articulation of the revisionist claim that:

> . . . nothing less than a proper understanding of those central
> beliefs--in "revelation," in "God," in "Jesus Christ"--can pro-
> vide an adequate understanding, a correct "reflective inventory,"
> or an existentially appropriate symbolic representation of the
> fundamental faith of secularity (9).

The key aspect of this claim is that Tracy first establishes
the "fundamental faith of secularity" and then tries to show
the "meaning and truth" of the central Christian symbols by
means of their correspondence to this faith (9). Clearly,
this is a bold apologetic *demonstratio christiana*.[47]

2) Negative Human Experience. Tracy's formulation of a
demonstratio christiana appeals primarily to a positive human
experience--the fundamental faith of secularity--as the proper
correlate of the Christian message. Conceivably, one could
utilize the same basic model of correlation while appealing
to a *negative* human experience (e.g., a need) as the proper
correlate. The closest representative of such an approach
would appear to be Paul Tillich's theology of correlation.[48]
As he summarizes it: "Theology formulates the questions
implied in human existence, and theology formulates the answers
implied in the divine self-manifestation under the guidance
of the questions implied in human existence" (61). Of interest
to us in this definition is the fact that human existence is
investigated with a view towards its questions or limitations
and that the correlation moves *from* the question *to* the answer.[49]

3) Ambiguous Human Experience. The most balanced approach
to a correlation of general human experience and Christian
revelation focuses on neither positive nor negative experience,
in exclusion from each other, but rather on the ambiguous
interrelationship of these two that is characteristic of real
life.[50] We previously noted a move in this direction in our

discussion of Bouillard's *demonstratio religiosa*. An example
within a specific *demonstratio christiana* can be found in
Eduard Schillebeeckx's discussion of a theological hermeneutics.[51]

Schillebeeckx understands theological hermeneutics to deal
with two basic problems: how can a Christian understand the
Christian message in the twentieth century, and how can she or
he justify the Christian interpretation of reality with regard
to modern thought (ix). The key to dealing with these problems
is located in the need to verify every dogmatic and theological
statement by a "hermeneutics of experience" *before* embarking on
a hermeneutics of Christian tradition (16). This "hermeneutics
of experience" proceeds by a method of correlation. To show
how this correlation works, however, Schillebeeckx first finds
it necessary to reformulate the method as it is usually understood (e.g., Tillich). In particular, he wants to emphasize
that our analysis of human existence reveals not only a negative
aspect--the constantly threatened *humanum* (91); it also reveals
a positive one--particular experiences which are signs or
glimpses of an ultimate meaning of human life (96). In light
of this analysis Schillebeeckx reformulates the correlation
as follows:

> Man, who, despite everything, is looking for meaning in the
> world, asks a question and he must first answer the question
> himself. Something of the wonder of man's existence which he
> is trying, despite everything to realize and which he . . .
> continues to trust in and commit himself to . . . can be dis-
> cerned in this human answer. . . . Man's hesitant answer to
> his own question . . . is identified in Christian faith (99-100).

For Schillebeeckx the correlation moves *from* human experience
to Christian revelation, but the ambiguous nature of this
experience is explicitly recognized.

  b. *Christian Revelation - General Human Nature*. The typical
criticism of the first formulation of correlation--*from* human
experience *to* revelation--is that it makes human experience the
ultimate criterion of the legitimacy or meaning of revelation.[52]
In addition, Karl Barth has argued that the only effective
apologetics is one that simply "happens"--without advance

planning--when Christian revelation is proclaimed.[53] These
criticisms form the basis for the contrasting formulation of
the method of correlation which stresses the movement *from*
Christian revelation *to* general human experience.[54] Most of
the theologians who stress this approach may be described as
hermeneutical fundamental theologians. We will consider Eugen
Biser as representative of this group.[55]

Biser constructs his approach in light of what he considers
to be the "Copernican turn" in fundamental theology. By this
phrase he means the resolve of certain fundamental theologians
(notably, Karl Adam), who were convinced that one could never
be brought to faith through rational or existential argumentation, to "seek the starting point for the grounding of faith
in faith itself"(52). Accordingly, Biser designates the
proclamation of the saving message as the place where the
apologetic interest is most efficiently fulfilled (58). What
is fundamental theology's role in relation to this proclamation?
Essentially, it is twofold: first, the fundamental theologian
must undertake a structural analysis of faith that shows it to
be a *Credere Deum Deo*--i.e., a self-grounding mode of understanding (55, 62-65); and second, the fundamental theologian
must obtain a precise determination of the *Zeitgeist* of his or
her setting (170). The latter task is necessary because Biser
ultimately focuses the task of fundamental theology in establishing an "understanding of faith" (hence the title of the
book) through a dialogue between faith and the world (6-7).
He explicitly contrasts this with an "apologetic for faith,"
which he sees as moving from experience to faith rather than
from faith to experience (23). Thus, Biser's *demonstratio
christiana* starts with self-grounded Christian faith and seeks
to awaken an understanding of this faith among nonbelievers
through a dialogue with the contemporary *Zeitgeist*.[56]

c. *Circular Relationship of the Correlates*. If the method
of correlation is to work effectively, then it is important to
recognize the unfruitfulness of unduly separating the previous
two formulations. Just as the first approach is in danger of
making experience the judge of revelation, the second is in
danger of not taking experience seriously enough and thereby

formulating revelation in unmeaningful terms. What is needed
is a deeper appreciation of the often mentioned, but seldom
developed, circular relationship between the investigation of
revelation and that of general human experience. It is important to realize that 1) the fundamental theologian's sensitivity
to the perspective of faith may well make her or him cognizant
of aspects of human reality that, while present, are not readily
evident to nonbelievers; and 2) a fundamental-theological
investigation of general human experience may well provide a
new perspective for assessing the meaning of faith and helping
to determine what is essential to faith.[57] A truly adequate
demonstratio christiana should move *both* from faith to experience and from experience to faith.[58]

2. Comparative Religions Analysis of Christianity's Claims

A distinctive alternative to a *demonstratio christiana* that
proceeds by a correlation of revelation and experience is one
that examines Christianity's claim to be *the* authentic revelation through a comparison with the other religions of the world.
While several theologians have addressed this issue in passing,
there have been very few contemporary[59] attempts to develop a
full *demonstratio christiana* from this perspective--partly, no
doubt, because of the immensity of such an undertaking. The
most significant contemporary example of such an approach are
the programmatic observations of Wolfhart Pannenberg concerning
a theology of religions.[60]

Pannenberg understands theology to be a science of the
historic religions because it is in these religions that theology's object--God--has been expressed (310-14). As such,
Christian theology is one particular type of theology among
others (325). Its task is the study of the Christian religion
(314). It is in this context of competing theologies that the
question of Christianity's claim to divine revelation must be
faced. Pannenberg rejects any mere confessional affirmation of
this claim as lacking intellectual legitimation (323). Instead,
he asserts the need to base *Christian* theology on a fundamental
theology (which is apparently transconfessional), whose task is
to define the particularity of the Christian revelation in the
context of the general problematic of religion (325). In this

fundamental theology the superiority of Christianity is not
assumed but rather becomes the explicit object of investigation (323).

This fundamental theology would be comprised of two basic
steps. First, there would be a philosophy of religion, which
would construct the general concept of religion and introduce
the idea of God into that context (367-68).[61] Second, a history
of religions would translate the abstract concept of religion
developed in the philosophy of religion into the historic
reality of religious life (369). Through these two steps we
would arrive at a determination of the relationship of Christianity and other religions.

Somewhat surprisingly, Pannenberg disavows any apologetic
function in this fundamental theology (370). Its function is
not to determine the truth of Christianity but rather only to
provide a provisional location of Christianity within the
historical world of religions (417). This disavowal must,
however, be read in light of Pannenberg's understanding of the
historical nature of revelation and truth. Final truth can
only be determined at the end of history. Therefore, a fundamental theology could only determine the ultimate truth of
Christianity in light of eschatological history (417). Until
that time, it must content itself with a provisional report
on the current status of Christianity vis-a-vis the other
religions.[62]

C. *Demonstratio Ecclesiastica*

The third step of classical apologetics was devoted to
demonstrating the validity of the claim of a particular tradition (Catholic or Protestant) to be the authoritative source,
mediator, or preserver of the Christian revelation. One evidence
of the move towards an ecumenical fundamental theology is that
a number of theologians have discarded, or radically altered,
any such reflection in their program.[63]

Our concern in this section is not to discuss such limitations but rather to reflect on a unique fundamental-theological
role that certain theologians have recently ascribed to a
demonstratio ecclesiastica. For these theologians fundamental-
theological reflection on the Church is not a mere appendage

to the *demonstratio religiosa* and *demonstratio christiana*,
charged with defending the claims of a particular confession.
Rather, it is viewed as the indispensable core of an effective
fundamental theology. That is, they argue that any attempt to
ground faith that does not make reflection on the Church a
central step in its procedure will fail. A mere *demonstratio
religiosa* or *christiana* alone is not sufficient. We will
consider three significant advocates of this approach in terms
of how they see the relation of the *demonstratio ecclesiastica*
to the other steps of fundamental theology.

1. Religiosa - Ecclesiastica - Christiana

Heimo Dolch[64] follows Bouillard in defining the goal of
fundamental theology as showing the correlation of Christianity
and human existence (31) and in locating the starting point of
fundamental theology in experience (29). However, he rejects
Bouillard's starting point of general human experience as too
indeterminate. Instead, we need a concrete experience (30),
which he defines as "God's constant and affirming faithfulness
in carrying out the divine plan of salvation"(33). Accordingly,
the proper way to ground faith is to give a phenomenological
analysis of God's acts and God's people through history. This
analysis would have two steps. First, one would reflect on the
fate (e.g., Auschwitz) and self-understanding of the Jewish
people, emphasizing their unbelievable trust in God's guidance
(34). This would constitute a type of *demonstratio religiosa*
via induction (36fn25). Next, we would move to an analysis of
concrete events in the life of the Christian Church (e.g.,
Vatican II) to show that these are unique events unlike any
other (38). This would constitute a *demonstratio ecclesiastica*.
Only then could we engage in a *demonstratio christiana*, which
would seek to determine the identity of this Jesus Christ whom
the community calls Lord (39). Throughout, Dolch's emphasis
is that a concrete approach focused on a particular community
of God's people can more effectively ground faith than the
"abstract" positions previously summarized.

2. Ecclesiastica - Christiana - Religiosa

Adolf Kolping is in the midst of constructing a fundamental
theology that he understands to be in sympathy with Dolch (84).[65]
The goal of his project is to show the credibility of the revelation proclaimed by the Church (9). His hope is that such
fundamental-theological reflection will give prospective
believers a new perspective on the Church whereby they can
recognize it as the messenger of God (85). To effectively
achieve this result, fundamental theology must undertake an
analysis of the present day Church because it is in this
Church that we actually experience the economy of salvation (84).
This analysis would seek to establish the signs of divinity
in the Church and to demonstrate the credibility of the Church's
claim to reveal God's word (35).[66]

In light of his understanding of its task, we would agree
with Platzer that Kolping has written his fundamental theology
in the reverse order of his argument. His real order of argument appears to run: Because the present-day Church can be
shown to be the witness of God (*demonstratio ecclesiastica*),
there must be means of showing it was established by divine
initiative in Jesus Christ (*demonstratio christiana*). If this
is possible, then the human has been shown to be open to such
initiative (*demonstratio religiosa*).[67]

3. Ecclesiastica - Religiosa and Christiana

An intriguing formulation of a *demonstratio ecclesiastica*
has been developed by the Protestant Edward Farley under the
heading of phenomenological theology.[68] Farley formulates his
phenomenological theology as a response to Feuerbach's challenge
that there is no transcendent reality behind the language of
the Christian faith (6). His guiding contention is that "the
corporate historical existence which entered the world in and
through Jesus of Nazareth (ecclesia[69]) involves reality-
references and reality-apprehensions[70] . . . in the pre-reflective, pre-institutional strata of this community"(xiii). To
gain access to these apprehensions, Farley employs the methods
and gains of social phenomenology to develop a phenomenological
theology. The first step of such a theology would be a

"theological *epoché*," i.e., one would suspend commitment to all
theological authorities and metaphysical schemes (71). What
remains for theology to consider after this *epoché* is "the
matrix of reality-apprehensions of the community of faith"(71).
Such apprehensions are fundamentally evident and thus not subject to further confirmation or disconfirmation (66). They are
the base upon which theology can build.

Having established this base, phenomenological theology
proceeds to render explicit the contours, the essence and the
modes of existence that lie present but hidden in faith's
reality-apprehensions (23). Here a second major contention of
Farley comes into play--namely, that the reality-apprehensions
of faith present not only themselves but "appresent" other
realities (217).[71] Importantly, he includes the notions of a
historical redeemer (217) and the transcendent (223) among
these realities. With this contention the direction of Farley's
argument becomes clear: If one will engage in a phenomenological investigation of the ecclesia (*demonstratio ecclesiastica*),
one will find implicit in the fundamentally evident reality-
apprehensions of this ecclesia the basis for affirming a
historical redeemer (*demonstratio christiana*) and the reality
of the transcendent (*demonstratio religiosa*).[72]

D. *Emphasis on Conversion*

We turn our attention now to a group of theologians who are
increasingly critical of most of the approaches presented so
far. Their main complaint is that the previous approaches are
too rationalistic and not really conducive to conversion.[73]
Symptomatic of this rationalistic slant is the fact that many
of them try to validate theological claims "objectively"
rather than acknowledging and developing the role that conversion
plays in the recognition of these claims.[74] By contrast, the
theologians now to be considered understand fundamental theology as a reflection on the structures of Christian conversion,
with the aim of showing that the decision to become a Christian
can be a responsible exercise of human freedom.[75] The growing
influence of this approach is witnessed by the assertion of
one reviewer that the formulation of conversion theories has
become the distinctive mark of fundamental theology today.[76]

To gain an understanding of this approach, we will consider
two of its representatives: Louis Monden and Donald Gelpi.

Louis Monden's concern in a fundamental theology is to determine the possibility of contemporary belief.[77] He considers
the proper method of making this determination to be a self-
reflection of the believing subject (9). The fundamental
theologian deals with such questions as: "What happens when I
believe?" or "What, how and why can I, as a thoughtful person,
believe in our day and age?" Consideration of such questions
will reveal that the real motives of faith are pre-reflective.
The task of fundamental theology is to raise these motives to
the level of reflection and clarify their meaning and connection (11).[78] By so doing, the fundamental theologian will be
providing a basis for contemporary faith.

Donald Gelpi has produced the most developed example of a
fundamental theology that centers on conversion.[79] He defines
its task as the elaboration of a normative and comprehensive
theory of conversion (47). Drawing on Lonergan, he further
specifies this task as the development of three nests of categories which are needed to interpret any conversion experience:
1) a set of categories dealing with the manifold nature of
general human experience, 2) a set of general theological categories that give a normative description of the process and
motives of conversion, and 3) a set of specific categories
that permit one to situate specific kinds of religious experience within one's general theory of conversion (45-47). A
special concern of Gelpi, developed in critical dialogue with
Lonergan, is the role and cognitive claims of emotion in
conversion (45). Throughout, the goal of his articulation of
the structures of conversion is to show the ground for a
religious tradition (393).[80]

Despite their quite different methodologies, Monden and
Gelpi are agreed that faith is most effectively grounded
through an analysis of the process and motives of conversion.

E. *Rahner's Foundational Course*

Karl Rahner's recent reflection has centered on the need for
and nature of a foundational course (*Grundkurs*) in theology.
His awareness of the need for such a discipline developed

through reflection on the problematic role of fundamental
theology in Catholic theological education.[81] Fundamental
theology (*Fundamentaltheologie*) was understood as a critical
and systematic reflection upon the grounds of credibility of
Christian revelation and the obligation of faith.[82] This
reflection had to deal with everything that was given as content or reasons in the total statement of faith (125).
Beginning theological students were instructed in such a
fundamental theology with the goal of being able to construct
a personal fundamental theology which could serve as a self-
conscious critical basis for their faith. The problem that
Rahner noted was that such a goal was unrealistic. It presup-
posed a far greater acquaintance with the individual theological
disciplines than was possible for even accomplished theologians,
let alone beginning students (115-16). On the other hand, the
students do need a basis for their faith (119). How could
this basis be provided?

The key to Rahner's answer to this question is his distinction between two types of justification of faith: comprehensive,
self-critical justification and unreflected "lived" justification (125). The first of these was the ideal aimed at in
traditional fundamental theology. It is a possibility, at best,
for only a select group of theologians. On the other hand, the
very existence of faith among contemporary persons of average
intellectual capacity shows that there must be another,
unreflected type of justification because faith--to be morally
acceptable--must be justified (124-25).[83] It is upon this
originally unreflected but "lived" justification of faith that
Rahner proposes to build his foundational course. The task of
the latter will be to locate and methodically reflect upon this
unreflective justification (125). Such reflection will determine the "sufficient" basis for an intellectually respectable
faith, as opposed to fundamental theology's concern to provide
a "comprehensive" basis (125).[84]

In light of this distinction, Rahner characterizes his
completed foundational course[85] as a first level of reflection
which aims at an intellectually honest affirmation of Christian
faith, without having to conduct a scientifically exact and
complete investigation of all the theological disciplines (6).[86]

The starting point for this foundational course is actual lived faith. Its goal is to provide the believer with confidence in the intellectual honesty of his or her faith, on the basis of the very *content* of Christian belief (12). Accordingly, the foundational course must necessarily be a specific unity of fundamental theology and dogmatic theology (11).[87] The basic argument of the foundational course is comprised of three steps: first, there is reflection on human existence as the question it is; second, the transcendental and historical conditions which make revelation possible are considered; finally, attention is devoted to Christianity's assertion to be the answer to the question which constitutes human existence (11).[88]

The similarities between the structure of Rahner's foundational course and approaches to fundamental theology through correlation are striking. This leads us to the question of the uniqueness of Rahner's approach and its contribution to our larger project. The choice of the believing person as a starting point is not unique to Rahner. Likewise, the integration of the content of Christian belief into fundamental theological investigation is not unique. Indeed, we found both of these moves to be characteristic of the new setting of fundamental-theological discussion. What is unique to Rahner is the incorporation of realistic didactic considerations into the very description of the task of fundamental theology. Too many fundamental theologians define their project and carry out their reflections as if the only legitimate result of fundamental-theological investigation was a comprehensive, self-critical grounding of faith. Rahner has shown that the actual result of this style of reflection is that little or no real grounding of faith takes place. If fundamental theologians are to take their didactic task seriously, they must find ways of carrying out their reflections and presenting their results that are in tune with the different types of certainty to which Rahner has referred and that draw on the insights into the motives and processes of conversion emphasized in the previous section.

[1]E.g., Kolping, *Fundamentaltheologie*, I: 85.

[2]E.g., Karl Rahner, "Reflections on the Contemporary Intellectual Formation of Future Priests," *Theological Investigations VI*, (NY: Seabury, 1979), p. 125. Behind this realignment of emphasis is a deepened appreciation of the circular relationship between commitment and understanding--i.e., that commitment is rarely made without some understanding while, conversely, understanding can be facilitated and deepened through commitment.

[3]The word "religious" is enclosed in quotation marks because of the ambiguous nature of its meaning. Many theologians treated in this section, drawing on Barth and Bonhoeffer, are very critical of the traditional attempt to portray the human as a "religious" being. However, they are still concerned to portray an openness of the human to a dimension (or call--Ebeling) of Ultimacy that enables us to transcend our normal spiritual, social and ethical limits.

[4]Cf. in this regard, VanderMark's comment that the most striking characteristic of contemporary fundamental theology is its explicitly Christian origin and orientation. William VanderMark, "Fundamental Theology: A Bibliographical and Critical Survey," RelStR 8 (1982): 245.

[5]For the purposes of our discussion we will understand "apologetics" in the broad sense of the concern "to provide arguments that all reasonable persons, whether 'religiously involved' or not, can recognize as reasonable" (David Tracy, *The Analogical Imagination*, {NY: Crossroad, 1981}, p. 57). By contrast, a nonapologetic approach would not be aimed primarily at persuasion but rather at facilitating understanding. Obviously, the boundary between these two approaches is a fluid one, for the development of understanding is an integral part of persuasion. However, the distinction remains a helpful one to which we shall return in our critical summary (part three).

[6]Bouillard, "La Tâche actuelle," p. 15.

[7]*New Birth of Freedom*, (Phil.: Fortress, 1976), p. 114. N.B., Hodgson uses the title "foundational theology."

[8](Indianapolis: Bobbs Merrill, 1969). Page numbers in this paragraph refer to this book.

[9]Gilkey locates this dimension of ultimacy in our experiences of contingency and temporality. Some critics have charged that he does not really demonstrate the positive existence of this dimension; he only assumes its existence as a corollary of our "lack." If this is true, then Gilkey would belong among those we will treat as the negative approach to a *demonstratio religiosa*. However, we are taking him at his word in this survey. Cf. J. Wesley Robbins, "Professor Gilkey and Alternative Methods of Theological Construction," JR 52 (1972): 98.

[10]Gilkey, "Trends," pp. 155-56.

[11]For a critique of this distinction between meaning and truth see Robbins, "Professor Gilkey," p. 91.

[12](NY: Seabury, 1975), pp. 91-118.

[13]*Idea of God*, pp. 80-98. Page numbers refer to this essay. The developed form of these programmatic remarks is *What is Man?* (Phil.: Fortress, 1970). Pannenberg's discussion of anthropology is treated here instead of in the following section where we deal with the need for ontological reflection in the *demonstratio religiosa* because he purposively avoids such transcendental reflection. His anthropology is a conversation with the various anthropological sciences, not the construction of an ontology.

[14] Pannenberg, *What is Man?* p. 12.

[15] *Introduction to a Theological Theory of Language*, (Phil.: Fortress, 1973). Numbers in the next two paragraphs refer to this work.

[16] Gerhard Ebeling, *God and Word*, (Phil.: Fortress, 1967), p. 6.

[17] It is not surprising that these reflections on a theological theory of language have been characterized as a "covert apologetic." (Forrest Lammiman, "Theology and Theories of Language," Enc 33 {1972}: 409). Ebeling, however, claims that he is not trying to prove God but only to show what the word "God" means (*God and Word*, p. 26). His justification for this reply can best be seen in his claim that "the doctrine of law and gospel indicates how to relate the language of faith to the experience of the world in the appropriate way" (*Theory of Language*, p. 203). From this perspective, his theological theory of language becomes merely one explication of his more characteristic approach which we will treat under the section on a negative *demonstratio religiosa*.

[18] Detailed arguments for the necessity of this further step can be found in: William J. Hill, "Seeking Foundations for Faith: Symbolism of Person or Metaphysics of Being?" *Thomist* 45 (1981): 236-42; and Hansjürgen Verweyan, "Fundamentaltheologie - Hermeneutik - Erste Philosophie," ThPh 56 (1981): 358-88, esp. 359, 363.

[19] Gilkey, *Naming*, pp. 224-27.

[20] David Tracy, "Foundational Theology as a Contemporary Possibility," *Dunwoodie Review* 12 (1972): 4. Tracy understands this two-step procedure in fundamental theology to be the twin of a similar phenomenological/transcendental structure in contemporary (post-critical) philosophy. Ibid., p. 5.

[21] *Blessed Rage*, Chapter Seven: The Question of God: Metaphysics Revisited (146-71); and Chapter Eight: The Meaning, Meaningfulness, and Truth of God-Language (172-203).

[22] Schubert Odgen, "The Task of Philosophical Theology," in *The Future of Philosophical Theology*, ed. R. Evans, (Phil.: Westminster, 1971), pp. 144-68. Page numbers refer to this work. A development of these programmatic remarks can be found in Ogden, *Reality of God*.

[23] Ogden considers a further task of philosophical theology to be the assessment of the "credentials" submitted by the various candidate systems of revelation (72).

[24] David Tracy, *The Analogical Imagination*, (NY: Crossroad, 1981), pp. 161-63. A similar distinction appears to lie behind Ogden's description of his philosophical theology as being "post-critical." Ogden, "Philosophical Theology," p. 71.

[25] Ontology is normally differentiated from metaphysics on the basis that it focuses on the meaning of reality in terms of its relation to the human. That is, it deals with the "limit-of" as the correlate to the "limit-to."

[26] (NY: Seabury, 1969). Page numbers in this paragraph refer to this edition.

[27] A detailed analysis of Rahner's understanding of the supernatural existential can be found in Kenneth Eberhard, *Karl Rahner's Doctrine of the Supernatural Existential*, (Ann Arbor, MI: University Microfilms, 1971).

[28]*Ecclesial Man*, p. 72. He defines Catholic fundamental theology as "an analysis of the human condition of the act of faith and the predisposition of man towards revelation." Ibid., p. 249. He refers to Rahner's *Hearers of the Word* as the definitive expression.

[29]A unique aspect of Farley's conception of fundamental theology is that its function is not to facilitate the move from general experience to particular Christian experience but rather the move from his analysis of ecclesia to his analysis of human existence (139). This move from *demonstratio ecclesiastica* to *demonstratio religiosa* will be clarifed in the third section of this chapter.

[30]*Fundamental Theology*, pp. 22-23.

[31]*Unfinished Man and the Imagination*, (NY: Seabury, 1968).

[32]John Macquarrie's discussion of philosophical theology reflects a similar approach. He sees the latter starting with given human existence (with its religious aspects) and trying to draw attention to those structures that lie at the root of religion and the life of faith. *Principles*, p. 58.

[33]Ebeling, "Fundamentaltheologie," pp. 510-11.

[34]Ibid., pp. 511, 517.

[35]Our analysis of this negative *demonstratio religiosa* is inherently a critique of the assertion of some Catholic theologians that Ebeling refuses to deal with a grounding of faith in fundamental theology. Cf. Pesch, "Fundamentaltheologie," p. 454.

[36]Gerhard Ebeling, "Reflections on Speaking Responsibly of God," *Word and Faith*, (Phil.: Fortress, 1963), pp. 333-53. Page numbers in this paragraph refer to this article.

[37]The similarities between Ebeling's approach and Catholic fundamental theology as epitomized in Aquinas have been frequently noted. (Cf. Schillebeeckx, *Revelation and Theology*, p. 82). Ebeling admits some similarities but sees his approach as focusing more on the problems of personal being than Aquinas (349).

[38]Gerhard Ebeling, "Theology and the Evidentness of the Ethical," JThC 2 (1965): 96-129. German original: "Die Evidenz des Ethischen und die Theologie," *Wort und Glaube II*, (Tübingen: J.C.B. Mohr, 1969), pp. 1-41. Page references in this paragraph are to the English edition.

[39]A detailed critique of Ebeling's attempt to base theology on ethics can be found in Wolfhart Pannenberg, *Ethics*, (Phil.: Westminster, 1981), pp. 57-86. Pannenberg's main complaint is that the contemporary radical criticism of all norms has made it impossible to speak of an "evidentness" and authority of the ethical. Ibid., pp. 72-73. A theological criticism of the extreme law/gospel distinction upon which Ebeling bases his approach can be found in Wilhelm Anderson, *Der Gesetzbegriff in der gegenwärtigen theologischen Diskussion*, (Munich: Chr. Kaiser, 1963).

[40]See especially, "La Tâche actuelle." Page references in next two paragraphs refer to this work.

[41]As this sentence suggests, Bouillard's approach is very closely related to the method of correlation that will be treated as a type of *demonstratio christiana*. However, his emphasis is on the presupposition that makes this correlation possible rather than the correlation itself. Accordingly, we are treating him here.

[42]Ebeling, "Evidentness of the Ethical," p. 125.

[43]Gilkey, *Naming*, p. 413.

[44]Ibid., pp. 450-51. Cf. Gilkey, "Trends," p. 155. It should be noted, however, that this distinction begins to blur in Gilkey's recent book *Reaping the Whirlwind*. He claims there that the prolegomenon should also relate traditional (Christian) symbols to life experiences—a role that is not only a preparation for constructive theology but also an intrinsic part of it (144). He adds in a footnote, however, that the ultimate correlation takes place not at the level of prolegomenon or fundamental theology but rather at the level of constructive theology (373fn1).

[45]Cf. Tracy's claim that by warranting a "religious" dimension in human existence the fundamental theologian has also warranted the possibility of entering into conversation with a given religion. *Analogical Imagination*, p. 163.

[46]Tracy, *Blessed Rage*. Page numbers in next five paragraphs refer to this work.

[47]In fairness to Tracy it should be noted that he seems to speak with "softer" apologetic tones in his more recent works. In particular, he now stresses a distinction between fundamental theology, which warrants the claims to truth of the religious dimension of human existence, and systematic theology, which warrants the claim to truth of *a concrete religion* (*Analogical Imagination*, p. 198. This distinction is barely distinguishable from that of Gilkey in *Reaping*). An intriguing insight into the results of this shift in Tracy's stance can be found in his recent description of the basic strategy of *Blessed Rage for Order*. He now defines this strategy as the attempt to show 1) that a religious interpretation of our common human experience is *meaningful and true*; 2) that belief in God as the proper referent of that religious experience and language is *meaningful and true*; and 3) that, within this religious and theistic frame of reference, it is *meaningful* to appeal to the particularity of the Christian event of Jesus Christ ("Defending the Public Character of Theology," p. 352, emphasis added). Of interest in this description is that, in contrast to the claims regarding the religious dimension of human existence and God, fundamental-theological claims about Christ are defended only as *meaningful*, not as *true*. The latter defense would now be a task of systematics. This distinction is not made in *Blessed Rage for Order* itself.

[48]Tillich, *Systematic Theology*, I: 59-66. If Ebeling were to develop an explicit *demonstratio christiana*, it would probably take this form.

[49]It has properly been questioned whether this is really a theory of correlation since the first analysis deals only with questions and the second only with answers. Tracy, for example, has characterized Tillich's method as one of juxtaposition rather than correlation. *Blessed Rage*, p. 46.

[50]Cf. in this regard, Tracy's recent reservations about the overly "positive" tone of *Blessed Rage for Order*, and his acceptance of the need to treat the negativities of human existence in a fundamental theology. "Public Character of Theology," p. 355.

[51]Eduard Schillebeeckx, *The Understanding of Faith*, (NY: Seabury, 1974). Page numbers in next paragraph refer to this work.

[52]E.g., Avery Dulles, "Method in Fundamental Theology: Refections on David Tracy's *Blessed Rage for Order*," TS 37 (1976): 310.

[53]Barth, *Church Dogmatics*, I.1: 30.

[54]It should be noted that most of these theologians see such a *demonstratio christiana* as the starting point of fundamental theology. They tend to consider a *demonstratio religiosa* as either illegitimate or as implied in their analysis of a given revelation.

[55]Eugen Biser, *Glaubensverständnis. Grundriss einer hermeneutischen Fundamentaltheologie*. (Freiburg: Herder, 1975). Page numbers in next paragraph refer to this work.

[56]A similar approach is evident in Bernd Jochen Hilberath, *Theologie zwischen Tradition und Kritik*, (Düsseldorf: Patmos, 1978). He defines fundamental theology as "hermeneutic" in the sense that, "starting from the revelation of God in Jesus Christ, it builds a bridge between the 'signs of the times' and the fundamental-theological structures and assertions" (328). A detailed critique of Biser, from a more apologetic viewpoint, can be found in Josef Meyer zu Schlochtern, "Verständigung über den Glauben. Anmerkungen zu Bisers Fundamentaltheologie," TThZ 85 (1976): 344-56.

[57]Cf. Rahner's claim that a correlation of experience and Christian dogma can help establish a valid hierarchy of the truths of faith. Karl Rahner, *Theological Investigations XVI*, (NY: Crossroad, 1979), p. 10.

[58]This emphasis on the dialogical relationship between fundamental-theological knowledge and extratheological human experience will be a central element of our constructive proposal in part three.

[59]It should be noted that this type of *demonstratio christiana* was a very common approach in the nineteenth century. A good example is the observations of Friedrich Schleiermacher concerning the supremacy of Christian piety over all other forms of piety (*The Christian Faith*, {Phil.: Fortress, 1976}, pp. 31-52). The very brevity of these observations suggests why this style of *demonstratio christiana* declined in more recent theological discussion--namely, the apparent ease with which Schleiermacher could demonstrate the superiority of Christianity as a direct corollary of the deficiency of his exposure to and intimate knowledge of other faiths. The more we have learned of these faiths, the more difficult--and thus more rare--such projects have become.

[60]Pannenberg, *Theology and the Philosophy of Science*. Page numbers in next three paragraphs refer to this work. Pannenberg has not yet developed a concrete explication of the program he describes.

[61]Note that Pannenberg understands this philosophy of religion to require a general anthropology as a basis. We treated his understanding of such an anthropology above in the section on *demonstratio religiosa*.

[62]This emphasis on the provisional nature of the results of such an approach to a *demonstratio christiana* highlights its limitations. Such an inclusive investigation would never end and could never really ground either faith or theology. As an ideal goal it is suggestive of corrections to other approaches. As a concrete formulation of a practical methodology it is suspect.

[63]Among Catholics see especially: Tracy, Biser and O'Collins; among Protestants: Gilkey, Pannenberg and Ebeling.

[64]Der systematische Ort der Kirche. Zur Frage des Ausgangspunktes und der Methode der Fundamentaltheologie," in *Volk Gottes. Festgabe für J. Höfer*, (Freiburg: Herder, 1967), pp. 28-40.

[65]*Fundamentaltheologie. Bd. I, Theorie der Glaubwürdigkeitserkenntnis der Offenbarung* (1968). *Bd. II, Die konkretgeschichtliche Offenbarung Gottes* (1974). *Bd. III, Die katholische Kirche als die Sachwalterin der Offenbarung Gottes. I. Teil: Die geschichtlichen anfänge der Kirche Christi* (1981). (Münster: Regensberg Verlag).

[66]Details on how this analysis would proceed are only now coming forth with the recent publication of the first part of his specific treatment of the Church, which deals with its origins.

[67]Cf. F. Platzer, "Zu einem Entwurf der Fundamentaltheologie," *Theologie der Gegenwart* 18 (1975): 165-70.

[68]*Ecclesial Man*, (Phil.: Fortress, 1975).

[69]Farley distinguishes ecclesia as an intersubjectively shaped redemptive consciousness from "church" with its sectarian connotations (xiv).

[70]An apprehension is a type of immediate awareness in which evidence occurs in its most individual and basal form. See his discussion of this term on pp. 65-68.

[71]Farley understands apperception (the awareness of appresented realities) as an intuitive awareness of objects copresent in immediate apprehensions (199). See his detailed discussion of this concept on pp. 194-203.

[72]A good criticism of the central claims of Farley's proposal can be found in Gordon Kaufman, "Review of *Ecclesial Man*," RelStR 2.4 (1976): 10-13. Unfortunately, Farley does not develop further the truth status of appresented realities in his sequel *Ecclesial Reflection*, (Phil.: Fortress, 1982) (see p. xix). This is a serious omission in light of the crucial role the notion of apprehension plays in his work.

[73]E.g., Avery Dulles, "Fundamental Theology and the Dynamics of Conversion," *Thomist* 45 (1981): 177.

[74]Cf. William J. O'Brien, "A Methodological Flaw in Tracy's Revisionist Theology," *Horizons* 5 (1978): 175-84.

[75]Dulles, "Dynamics of Conversion," p. 176.

[76]Matthias Neumann, The Role of Imagination in the Tasks of Fundamental Theology," Enc 42 (1981): 314.

[77]*Faith: Can Man Still Believe?* (NY: Sheed & Ward, 1970).

[78]Significantly, the reflective justification of faith is expressly discounted as being itself a motive of faith (36). Thus, such a reflective justification would not constitute the core of a fundamental theology. While Monden includes the justification of faith as part of his fundamental theology, it is dependent upon the section that analyzes the motives of faith (11).

[79]*Experiencing God*, (NY: Paulist Press, 1978). N.B., Gelpi uses the term "foundational theology."

[80]Gelpi appears to understand his project as a minor alteration of Lonergan's foundational theology. In reality, he changes the very focus of the discipline, for his concern focuses on the grounding of a religious tradition (393) while Lonergan's concern focuses on grounding the enterprise of doctrinal theology.

[81]Karl Rahner, "Reflections on the Contemporary Intellectual Formation of Future Priests," *Theological Investigations VI*, (NY: Seabury, 1969), pp. 113-38. Page references in next two paragraphs are to this article.

[82]Karl Rahner, "Reflections on a New Task for Fundamental Theology," *Theological Investigations XVI*, (NY: Seabury, 1979), p. 156.

[83]This assertion of the necessity for faith to be justified appears to be significantly qualified in Rahner's recent recognition of the lack of an immediate awareness of the reasons for faith. The point remains, however, for he still holds that these reasons can be manifested--albeit by an indirect method. Cf. Rahner, "New Task," p. 159.

[84]Rahner further clarified this distinction recently by appealing to St. Ignatius' differentiation between the first and second times of choice in faith as a corollary to the two types of justification of faith he has in view. The first level of justification would represent that point at which one has obtained a "manageable" grasp of the reasons and motives of an absolute decision. The second level would be the ideal of a comprehensive grasp, obtainable only after years of reflection. Rahner, "New Task," p. 161.

[85]*Foundations of Christian Faith*, (NY: Seabury, 1978). Page references in this paragraph refer to this work.

[86]The latter task would be assigned to a second level of reflection (9) which would include a fundamental theology. The foundational course would serve as a prelude to this second level (14).

[87]Rahner is apparently using fundamental theology (*Fundamentaltheologie*) here as a reference to the traditional discipline which is purely formalistic--i.e., abstracted from the content of faith (cf. p. 12). He has himself argued elsewhere that this fundamental theology itself must be more closely linked with dogmatics ("Fundamental Theology," in *Theological Dictionary*, eds. K. Rahner & H. Vorgrimler, {NY: Herder, 1965}, pp. 181-82). Thus, the closer tie to dogmatics is not, in itself, the distinctive difference between fundamental theology and the foundational course.

[88]Peter Knauer has presented an ecumenical fundamental theology (*Der Glaube kommt vom Hören*, {Cologne: Styria, 1977}) which he understands to be a foundational course in Rahner's sense (9). In terms of starting with a given faith stance he does agree with Rahner (11). However, he does not try to ground faith through a correlation of human existence and Christian revelation. Rather, he concentrates on explicating the Christian message. Characteristic of Knauer is the claim that the credibility of the Christian message can only be grasped in faith itself (314). The only "argumentative" grounding he presents for faith are the negative arguments that 1) faith can be believed because it cannot be projected from reason (242), and 2) unbelief can be shown to be arbitrary while belief cannot so the choice between belief and unbelief is not a choice between equals (283).

CHAPTER FIVE
FUNDAMENTAL THEOLOGY AS
GROUNDING THEOLOGY

In the previous chapter we dealt with conceptions of fundamental theology that construed its primary goal as the provision
of a basis or grounding for Christian faith. We turn now to a
significantly different set of conceptions of fundamental theology, those which construe its primary task as providing the
justification or basis for pursuing theology as conceptual
reflection on Christian faith.[1]

It should be noted at the outset that the representatives
of this approach are not as widespread as the representatives
of the first approach. Neither have the formulations of this
approach reached a level of refinement and detail characteristic
of the formulations of fundamental theology as grounding faith.
The primary reason for this is that the incorporation of the
task of grounding theology in a fundamental theology is a
relatively recent event, particularly among Catholics. Also,
the current ferment in investigations concerning the nature and
method of theology has not yet settled enough to allow a precise
and comprehensive summary like that possible regarding the first
approach. Nonetheless, this is an important part of the current
discussion of fundamental theology and deserves our attention,
especially since one of our goals is to show the way fundamental
theology provides an integrative context for questions of theological method.

A survey of the various formulations of fundamental theology
as a discipline aimed at grounding theology reveals three
basic tasks that have been assigned to such a discipline. First,
there is the task of demonstrating the legitimacy *of* theology
in view of the doubts raised about its right to exist, both
within and outside of the Church. Second, there is the need to
insure legitimacy *in* theology through reflection on the proper

99

understanding of its nature and methods.[2] Finally, there is
the practical problem of opting for a particular approach to
theology in view of the number of approaches presently available.

A. *Demonstrate Legitimacy* of *Theology*

One way to provide a foundation for theology is to justify
its existence in view of those who question either the need for
or right to this existence. These attacks have usually come
from "outside" the Church. Occasionally, however, there have
been questions about the need for and legitimacy of theological
reflection within the Church as well.

1. Defense Against External Critique

The questions concerning theology that have been raised by
its external critics fall into two major groups: a) does the
subject matter with which theology claims to deal have an
"objective" reality, and b) can theology's mode of inquiry be
legitimately designated as scholarly or "scientific"?

a. *The Subject Matter of Theology*. The first way a fundamental theology could defend the legitimacy of theology is by
demonstrating the reality of its subject matter. This undertaking provides an excellent example of the relationship between the fundamental-theological task of grounding faith and
that of grounding theology. Many of the attempts to ground
faith which were summarized in the previous chapter can also
be seen, at least implicitly, as attempts to ground theology
by demonstrating the reality of its subject matter. Indeed,
for some theologians this relationship was explicit. For
example, Claude Geffré locates the specific function of fundamental theology in the provision of a critical vindication of
dogmatic theology *through* a transcendental analysis of the
human.[3] If one demonstrates that human existence contains an
openness to a meaningful encounter with transcendence, one would
also have demonstrated the right to existence of a discipline
that tried to reflect upon that encounter.

Another example of this interplay between grounding faith and
grounding theology is Edward Farley's discussion of what he

calls phenomenological theology.[4] Farley states explicitly
that his primary concern is to show that the subject matter of
theology has more than a phenomenal status (17). He considers
this demonstration to be more basic to grounding theology than
the problem of theological method (8). Thus, while his book
could be read as an attempt to ground faith by arguing that
faith's essential contents are appresent in its reality-
apprehensions (as we argued in chapter four), it may also be
read as an attempt to ground theology by showing that its
subject matter has more than a phenomenal status.[5]

Of course, one can also defend the "objective" nature of the
subject matter of theology without basing it on a *demonstratio
religiosa*. One way to do this is simply to define theology's
subject matter in such a way that its reality is obvious: e.g.,
the Bible, the history of the Church, or discourse about God
(abstracting from the question of its referent).[6] A sophisti-
cated example of this approach is apparent in David Tracy's
attempt to defend the truth status of the claims of systematic
theology by developing an understanding of the latter's object
as the "classic."[7] Tracy takes it as self-evident that classics
exist in every culture (107). He then proceeds to argue that
what we mean by naming certain texts, rituals, symbols, etc.,
"classics" is that "here we recognize nothing less than the
disclosure of a reality we cannot but name truth" (108). A
uniquely "religious classic" will especially warrant this
recognition because it discloses the whole of reality (163).
Tracy defines the subject matter of theology as just such religious classics--i.e., texts, rituals, symbols, etc., which
disclose the meaning of reality as a whole. The point to his
definition is that, since the experience of classics is not
limited to the religious sector but rather pervades all of
culture, the public status of religious classics must be respected (134). That is, the subject matter of theology has a
"public" status on par with the various other subject matters
present in a culture.

b. *The Mode of Inquiry of Theology*. The demonstration of
the reality of theology's subject matter does not, in itself,
constitute a complete demonstration of the legitimacy of

theology. Many critics grant that there is "something" with
which theology deals. However, for them the question remains
whether, given the nature of this object, theology can pursue
a mode of inquiry and formulate results that are intersubjectively meaningful. Usually this question is framed in terms of
whether theology can be considered a science.

Some theologians have rejected the legitimacy of this question. For them, the only proper question about the mode of
inquiry of theology is whether it is true to its object.[8] The
question of how this mode of inquiry might correspond to
other types is discounted. However, as we noted in the historical survey, this strong anti-apologetic tone of theology is
on the wane. Most contemporary theologians consider it
necessary to give an account of the mode of theological inquiry
that is at least understandable to other disciplines, if not in
correspondence with them. We will draw on two prominent par-
ticipants in the discussion of the "scientific" nature of
theology to illustrate this type of fundamental-theological
reflection--Gerhard Sauter and Wolfhart Pannenberg.

1) Gerhard Sauter has edited a book which surveys the
importance of the philosophy of science (*Wissenschaftstheorie*)
for theology.[9] The goal of the book is to show, in terms of
the philosophy of science, that theology is a meaningful realm
of endeavor (10). This demonstration is not executed in terms
of the object of theology but rather by considering theology's
procedures (234). Sauter maintains that theology can be shown
to deal with the three main concerns of all scholarly inquiry:
1) to establish a field of validity, 2) to distinguish between
scientific and ordinary discourse, and 3) to formulate its
results in logically valid sentences (9-13).[10] Therefore,
theology can claim the same type of legitimacy as any other
mode of inquiry.[11]

2) Wolfhart Pannenberg has also attempted to demonstrate the
scholarly character of theology through a conversation with the
philosophy of science.[12] His argument is more ambitious than
that of Sauter. He tries to show not only that theology's mode
of inquiry corresponds to that of other sciences (especially
the human sciences) but also that the existence of theology is
necessary for science to reach its goal of a unity of

knowledge (13). To demonstrate this, he presents an overview
of the historical development of the philosophy of science.
His aim is to show that there has been an increasing awareness
of the need for an inclusive framework for all knowledge and
meaning (cf. 102). All scientific knowledge aims at the ideal
of dealing with reality as a whole. At this juncture, Pannenberg draws on the sociology of religion to argue that it is
in religion that one finds the prevailing experience of reality
as a whole given expression (311-12). Therefore, for science
to reach its goal of a unity of knowledge, it requires theology
as the science of religion (314). Thus, for Pannenberg, the
scientific ideal not only allows for the discipline of theology,
it requires it.

2. Defense Against Internal Critique

Throughout the history of the Christian Church there have
been those who, in the name of the Gospel or the Christian
life, have questioned the legitimacy of theological reflection.
Their usual contention has been that there is a basic incongru-
ence between Christian faith and reflective reasoning. In this
light, many theologians have found it advisable, in the introduction to their theological endeavors,[13] to defend the
legitimacy of theological reflection through an analysis of
such problems as the relation of faith to reason or of authority
to criticism. The goal of these analyses is to show that
theological reflection is not merely appropriate for Christian
faith, it is a necessary part of the Christian concern to integrate faith with the whole of human life. Such analyses have
rightly been designated as exercises in fundamental theology.[14]

B. *Insure Legitimacy* in *Theology*

By far the predominate task assigned to fundamental theology
by theologians who understand this discipline as aimed at
grounding theology is that of facilitating the legitimate exercise of actual theological reflection. For some of these
theologians the defense of theology's right to existence is an
integral part of such a fundamental theology. For others, the
existence of theology is simply taken as a given. In either
case, their primary concern is to show how fundamental theology

can help theology as a whole to proceed in an appropriate manner.

Our task in this section is to gain an understanding of the nature and scope of the investigations that have been considered integral to fulfilling this task of insuring legitimacy *in* theology. As throughout this essay, we will not devote extensive consideration to the answers that individual theologians have proposed for the questions involved in insuring legitimacy *in* theology. Rather, we will attempt to gain an appreciation of what the relevant questions are so that we may attain greater clarity concerning the task of fundamental theology. Of particular interest, in light of the lack of systematic treatments of these issues mentioned at the beginning of this chapter, will be the question of the scope of relevant areas of investigation when one wants to insure legitimacy *in* theology.[15]

The areas of investigation that have been designated as integral to the task of insuring legitimacy *in* theology can be grouped under two headings: 1) those aimed at determining theology's nature, and 2) those aimed at determining the appropriate methods of theology.

1. The Nature of Theology

In terms of the determination of theology's nature, areas of investigation that have been assigned to a fundamental theology include: theology's a) task, b) subject matter, c) sources, d) language, and e) basic categories.

a. *The Task of Theology*. The first problem normally assigned to a theological grounding discipline is the determination of the task and goal of theological reflection. Central to this problem is the determination of the relation of theology and faith.[16] Does theology merely explicate faith? Does it engage in critical reflection on faith? Or again, does it try to "ground" faith.[17]

As Stirnimann notes, this determination of the task and goal of theological reflection is essentially an epistemological undertaking.[18] To complete this undertaking one must not only reflect upon what the Church or tradition says about theology, one must also engage in a dialogue with contemporary

epistemological reflection. There are several recent examples
of such a dialogue.

Bernard Lonergan presented an ambitious attempt to determine
the task, encyclopedic division and methods of theological
reflection based on his own transcendental analysis of the
basic patterns of human cognition.[19] Wolfhart Pannenberg has
developed a conception of the task of theology as a science of
the historic religions through dialogue with the philosophy of
science.[20] Gerhard Sauter and Anton Grabner-Haider have formulated conceptions of the task of theology in particular dialogue
with analytic philosophy.[21] Finally, John Apczynski has presented an approach to theology based on the epistemological
reflections of Michael Polanyi.[22] The goal of each of these
investigations is to determine the task of theology and the
types of truth characteristic of theology.[23]

b. *The Subject Matter of Theology*. A second task typically
assigned to a theological grounding discipline is the determination of the subject matter or formal realm with which theology
deals.[24] As Sauter notes, such a determination is incumbent
on any discipline that is concerned with the clarity and
communicability of its reflections.[25] Among the alternative
designations of this subject matter that have found recent
representatives are: 1) the being of God, 2) faith, 3) the
beliefs and attitudes of a community, and 4) the Word of God.[26]
Central to all of these alternatives are the traditional questions of the nature of revelation and its relation to other
types of human experience.[27]

Obviously, the question of the subject matter of theology
must be explored in close correlation with the question of the
task of theology. It is not surprising, therefore, that recent
inquiries into this subject matter have also found it necessary
to enter into dialogue with contemporary epistemological and
ontological reflection. A good example is Theodore Jennings'
attempt to develop an understanding of the Christian "mythos"
as the subject matter of theology--an attempt which he admits
is formulated in dialogue with the new understandings of the
human as *homo symbolicum*.[28] Indeed, the question of the subject matter of theology is a constituent part--implicitly or

explicitly--of each of the descriptions of the task of theology
to which we referred above.

c. *The Sources of Theology*. A third undertaking that is
necessarily constitutive of reflection on the nature of theology
is the determination of the sources wherein theology's subject
matter can be apprehended.[29] Central to this undertaking will
be reflection on the character of Scripture, tradition and
general human experience.[30]

Once again, the determination of the sources of theology can
be effectively made only in close conjunction with the reflection on the task and subject matter of theology. A good
example of the interrelationship of these three problematics
in fundamental-theological reflection can be found in Gordon
Kaufman's *An Essay on Theological Method*.[31] The three central
contentions of his proposal for understanding the nature of
theology are: 1) that the proper subject matter of theology is
the concept of God (10); 2) that the proper task of theology is
the understanding, criticism, and--if necessary--reformulation
of this concept (37-39); and 3) that the sources from which
theology must draw in this task are not limited to religious
experience, but include the totality of language and tradition
that shape experience (6).

Despite this close correlation, the question of the sources
of theology should be preserved as a distinct moment of fundamental-theological reflection because one of the most
significant questions that will arise regarding the method of
theology is the relation of theology's subject matter to its
sources.

d. *The Language of Theology*. A particular focus of much
recent fundamental-theological reflection on the nature of
theology has been the question of religious and theological
language. While much of the work dealing with this question
has focused on determining the legitimacy *of* religious and
theological discourse,[32] there is an increasing concern to
investigate the importance of linguistic analysis for insuring
legitimacy *in* theological discourse.

Two distinctions have proven important in regard to the
latter concern. The first distinction is between ordinary
discourse and uniquely religious discourse such as God-talk or
mythology. The focus of concern in this distinction is to
isolate the unique ways in which religious discourse "means"
and, thereby, to gain more insight into the nature of the
subject matter and sources of theology.[33]

The second distinction is an inner-theological one between
primary performative speech acts and secondary theological
reflection.[34] This distinction corresponds to a general distinction in academic disciplines between ordinary discourse
and scholarly discourse.[35] The point of the distinction is
that the primary religious discourse provides the object of
the secondary theological reflection. The legitimacy of the
latter is therefore always derivative. It should never be
considered the goal of theology to replace the primary discourse
with secondary reflection. Likewise, the subject matter and
sources of theology should ultimately be located in such
primary discourse.

Extrapolating from the previous distinction, Stirnimann has
made a third distinction between theological discourse and meta-
theological discourse.[36] While theological discourse is
discourse about religious discourse, meta-theological discourse
is discourse about the "how" of theological discourse. That
is, it is the discourse of fundamental-theological reflection
on legitimacy *in* theology. Again, the point is that this discourse must recognize its derivative nature if theology is to
function legitimately.

e. *The Categories of Theology*. A final problem that some
have considered essential for a discipline that aims to provide
a foundation for subsequent theological thought is the development of a set of categories for theology. This emphasis has
taken three significantly different forms in recent discussion,
which can be summarized by considering their main representatives: Bernard Lonergan, Karl Rahner and Anders Nygren.

1) Bernard Lonergan's approach to the theological specialty
discipline he calls "foundational theology" is so distinctive
that this particular title has come to be identified with his

formulation.[37] For Lonergan, there is a twofold basis for the
theological task: the normative pattern of conscious and intentional human operations (19), and religious conversion as a
transformation of the subject (130). The first aspect of this
basis is common to all human reflection and is reflected on in
a general epistemology.[38] By contrast, conversion provides the
additional basis necessary for specifically Christian doctrinal
reflection. As such, the functional specialty of foundational
theology, which--within Lonergan's encyclopedic vision--is
obliged to provide the necessary foundations for the subsequent
specialties of doctrines, systematics and communications, is
assigned the task of developing the categories that will allow
one to explicate this conversion theologically (281). These
categories would deal with such topics as: individual religious subjectivity, communal service and worship, and the
possibility of progress or decline in religious commitment.
These categories are foundational in the sense that they provide the horizon within which the subsequent doctrines of
Christian theology can be apprehended (130).

2) Among Karl Rahner's formulations of fundamental-theological concerns is the discipline he has called "formal and
fundamental theology."[39] This discipline must be carefully
distinguished from both his fundamental theology found in
Hearers of the Word and his foundational course. Formal and
fundamental theology, unlike the other two, is entirely a constituent part of dogmatic theology. Its goal is not to ground
the entire theological enterprise but rather to analyze the
enduring formal structures of salvation history in a way that
can aid in the interpretation of this history in dogmatics.[40]
The focus of formal and fundamental theology is on the essence
of God and God's plan of salvation. In particular, it treats
such topics as: the fundamental relationship between God and
creatures, the concept of personal revelation, and the concept
of saving revelation. It would not only develop formal conceptions of these topics, it would strive to show phenomenologically
how concrete revelation has expressed these formal structures.[41]

Several fundamental theologians, drawing on Rahner, have
ascribed to fundamental theology per se the task of developing

the basic categories of theology. Among these categories they
normally include revelation, tradition, mystery, faith, etc.[42]

   3)   Anders Nygren has demonstrated the foundational nature
of motif research for the Lundensian approach to systematic
theology.[43] A religious motif is a unifying theme that is
characteristic of a particular religious tradition, apart from
which that tradition could not be interpreted.[44] One locates
a motif by immersing oneself in a tradition and pushing back
to the original presuppositions that give unity to views that
often appear contradictory on first consideration (354-56).[45]
Lundensian theology uses the fundamental motif of a religion
as the organizing principle for a systematic presentation of
that religion--i.e., a "theology" of that religion (12). As
such, motif research is fundamental for systematic theology in
that it provides the starting point and organizing principle
of the latter.

   Despite the differences of their various emphases, all three
approaches agree that an analysis of the themes or categories
of Christian faith is an essential part of providing the foundation for the formulations of doctrinal theology.

2. The Methods of Theology

   The second major group of tasks assigned to a fundamental
theology which strives to insure legitimacy *in* theology focuses
on the methods utilized in theological reflection. These questions of theological method fall into two major groups: a) those
pertaining to theological investigation, and b) those pertaining
to theological judgment. In addition, there is the overarching
methodological question of the encyclopedic unity of theology
(c). All of these questions of method are permeated by a basic
tension between two considerations. First, are these methods
appropriate to theology's subject matter? Second, are they
appropriate to the nature of general human inquiry?

   a. *Methods of Theological Investigation*. A central task
assigned to a theological grounding discipline is the determination of the appropriate methods of theological
investigation.[46] By theological investigation we mean the

endeavor to locate the subject matter of theology within the various sources of theology.

It is generally acknowledged that the methods of theological investigation will be consonant with or adapted from the methods of general human inquiry--historical, philosophical, psychological, etc. The decisive task of the fundamental theologian, in light of the basic tension in methodological reflection, is to determine the extent to which and manner in which the utilization of such "extratheological" methods is appropriate to theology's nature. Obviously, reflection on the nature of theology is a prerequisite for this determination. From this earlier reflection the fundamental theologian will seek basic principles to guide the development of methods for investigating theology's sources in a manner appropriate to its nature.[47]

An example of this type of reflection is Eduard Schillebeeckx's *Understanding of Faith*. In this book he engages in critical investigation of the various types of linguistic analysis--structural, phenomenological, logical and ontological (20-44)--and the new "critical theory" (102-155) to determine their possible contributions to a theological hermeneutic. His principle for adapting or rejecting aspects of the various methods is the question of whether they will allow the reality of what is offered as truth in the biblical message to manifest itself (32).

A similar reflection is evident in David Tracy's analysis of the role of phenomenological and transcendental reflection in dealing with those aspects of human experience that are relevant to theology and the role of hermeneutics in disclosing the central message of Scripture.[48] Reference could also be made to Langdon Gilkey's critical appropriation of the methods of linguistic analysis and phenomenology in his theological prolegomenon.[49]

b. *Methods of Theological Judgment*. The ultimate goal of theological reflection is not just to locate theologically relevant subject matter, it is to engage in normative theological judgments. As Friedrich Mildenberger notes, reflection ultimately becomes theological only when it includes the dogmatic-normative moment.[50] As such, a theological grounding

discipline must also reflect upon the means by which theology
executes its judgments concerning the legitimacy of particular
theological formulations. This reflection must deal with two
basic problems: 1) the criteria of theological argument, and
2) the structure of theological argument.

1) Criteria of Theological Argument. For any judgment to
take place, there must be criteria to which an argument can
appeal as warrant or backing. For example, to declare that
a particular ethical action is a theologically legitimate
action, one must have criteria that guide the judgment of
theological legitimacy. It is in light of this need that
theologians have assigned to fundamental theology the task of
articulating the criteria, warrants and backing of theological
argument.[51]

Traditionally, discussion of criteria has centered on the
issues of Scripture, dogma and ecclesial teaching office.[52]
At best, these criteria serve to show that a theological judgment is authentic to theology's sources. They do not, in
themselves, assure that the judgment is appropriate to general
human inquiry. To provide such an assurance, recent
fundamental-theological investigation has focused on developing
further criteria.

Anders Jeffner has provided a summary and analysis of
several such criteria appealed to in contemporary Protestant
German *Glaubenslehren*.[53] He locates four major types of criteria
operating--implicitly or explicitly--in these works. First,
there are the indirect criteria of Scripture, creed and faith
(30ff). These are the Protestant corollaries of the criteria
of authenticity referred to in the previous paragraph. Second,
there are criteria of experience, both general human experience
and special religious experience (63ff). Third, there are
scientific criteria--i.e., the probable results of scientific
inquiry (87ff).[54] Finally, there are logical criteria (98ff).
Jeffner does not blindly accept the legitimacy of all of these
criteria. Rather, he highlights the aporias that accompany
their use and suggests limitations that must be placed on certain of them, especially the second and third type, if they are
to be used in an argumentative theology (137).

2)   Structures of Theological Argument. To be legitimate,
a judgment must not only appeal to critically established
criteria, it must also utilize a valid argumentative structure.
Accordingly, the analysis and formulation of such a structure
for theological argument has been assigned to a discipline
concerned with legitimacy in theology.[55]

A central aspect of this particular task is the analysis
of the ways in which the claimed criteria of theological argument are actually used in theological judgments. An exemplary
model of such analysis is David Kelsey's survey of *The Uses of
Scripture in Recent Theology*.[56] He carefully illustrates the
variety of ways in which the criterion "Scripture" is appealed
to in actual theological argument. It is his hope that, by
making theologians conscious of the diverse ways in which such
criteria actually function, it will be possible to gain some
understanding of what it means to call upon any particular
criterion as an authority in a theological judgment (cf. 5).

As with the criteria of theological argument, an analysis
has been made of the actual argumentative structure utilized
in several recent Protestant systematic theologies, this time
by Koloman Micskey.[57] Micskey claims that a formal nine-point
axiom-system can be discerned as common to the theologians he
investigated: K. Barth, P. Tillich, W. Trillhaus and W. Pannenberg (115, 157).[58] Admittedly, the particular content ascribed
to the basic axioms differs from theologian to theologian.
Likewise, individual theologians devote more time to some
axioms than to others. Nevertheless, Micskey believes the
formal structure can be shown to be the same. Regardless of
how we assess this claim, the important point is that Micskey
illustrates the need for fundamental theologians to render the
underlying syntax of theological argument explicit and to seek
an agreement concerning this syntax (31).[59]

c. *The Unity of Theology*. A final methodological task
which has been assigned to a fundamental theology is that of
a theological encyclopedia--i.e., a consideration of the function and methods of the various subdisciplines of theology,
with special focus on their unity.[60] As Schubert Ogden notes,
the question of unity has become the most important aspect

of such an encyclopedic investigation because of the prolifer-
ation of theological specializations that is characteristic of
the contemporary setting.[61] Ironically, each of the three
major attempts to develop a theological encyclopedia has chosen
a different way to demonstrate this unity.

   1) Wolfhart Pannenberg has organized his theological encyclopedia[62] around the principle that the unity of the various
disciplines lies in their common object, not a common method
(297). Since this object is the revelation of God in the historic religions (314), the unity of the various disciplines is
found in their contribution towards understanding the history
of this revelation. It is in this light that Pannenberg
designates historical theology as the most comprehensive of
the theological disciplines (419).

   2) Gerhard Ebeling considers the overcoming of the split
between historical and systematic theology to be a primary
task of fundamental theology.[63] His proposal for overcoming
this split is to focus on the common hermeneutical concern of
the two disciplines. Indeed, he argues that the two disciplines
are simply two historically separate formulations of the one
hermeneutic task of theology--dogmatics being the classical
formulation and historical theology the contemporary one.[64]
This focus on the hermeneutical task of theology could conceivably be used to structure a systematic encyclopedia of
the various theological disciplines. Unfortunately, Ebeling
has not yet given such an account.[65]

   3) By far the most ambitious attempt to construct an
encyclopedic classification of the various theological disciplines is that of Bernard Lonergan.[66] Lonergan's model of the
eight specialty disciplines of theology--research, interpretation, history, dialectic, foundations, doctrines, systematics
and communications--is presented as a prescriptive model of
how the disciplines should be related, not a descriptive model
of how they actually function. The basis for this prescription
is his analysis of the foundational procedures of the human
mind, which uncovered the basic pattern of operations employed
in every cognitional enterprise (4). He uses this pattern to
develop an understanding of the number and nature of the theological disciplines, as well as their place in relation to each

other (133-35). Obviously, the legitimacy of this prescription
for the unity of theology is dependent upon the legitimacy of
both Lonergan's basic cognitional model and the applicability
of this model to theological work.[67]

C. *Selection of a Particular Conception of Theology*

We noted in our historical survey that a pluralism of
approaches to theology is a characteristic of the present
fundamental-theological discussion. The problem which this
poses for the fundamental theologian is the justification of
the decision for a particular approach as the most appropriate
one to use in developing constructive theological proposals.

Franz Schupp has devoted specific attention to this problem.[68]
He summarizes the situation of the contemporary theologian in
four points (35):

1. The pluralism of presently existing ideologies and theologies
    cannot be reduced to logically contradictory alternatives.

2. The complexity of certain of these alternative conceptions makes
    it impossible to present them adequately in all their respects.

3. As rational human beings, however, we must render a practical
    judgment over the probability of particular conceptions.

4. This judgment can be made only in light of concurring probabil-
    ities. However, the judgment of the greater probability of one
    conception does not (and cannot logically) lead to the falsity
    of another.

Schupp considers this situation to be the equivalent, in terms
of grounding theology, of the problem which Rahner addressed
with his foundational course, in terms of grounding faith.
Common to both situations is the demand for a decision in spite
of the fact that it cannot be comprehensively investigated or
defended.

In light of this situation, Schupp develops his own understanding of a foundational course, this time aimed at grounding
theology. Such a course would have three basic assignments.
First, it would acquaint its readers with the nature of the
problem summarized in his four-point analysis of the contemporary setting. Second, it would give a representative
introduction to the various alternative conceptions of theology.
Finally, and most importantly, it would advance and defend a
(provisional) choice for a particular conception (35). Based

on this fundamental-theological choice, the theologian could
then engage in constructive theological reflection.

[1]Gottlieb Söhngen's definition of fundamental theology is characteristic
of this approach: "Fundamental theology is that theological inquiry which
is obliged to pursue foundational reflection or investigation with the goal
of grounding theology as the science of revelation and faith." Söhngen,
"Fundamentaltheologie," p. 452.

[2]Obviously, these first two tasks are not mutually exclusive. In
particular, one of the central arguments in demonstrating the legitimacy
of theology is to show that there are means of insuring legitimacy *in*
theology.

[3]Geffré, "Recent Developments," p. 15.

[4]*Ecclesial Man*. Page numbers in this paragraph refer to this book.

[5]Farley's position on the truth status of the realities uncovered by
phenomenological theology is more complex than this summary might suggest.
He distinguishes between two senses of truth: first, what grounds theology--
i.e., shows that theology deals with "how the world is"; and second, how
can that ground be investigated in a way that will yield true judgments--i.e.,
the criteriological problem. (Cf. *Ecclesial Reflection*, pp. 304-5). His
point is that the phenomenological theology discussed in *Ecclesial Man* deals
only with the first sense--showing that theology has a transphenomenal basis
of religious knowledge. The task of *Ecclesial Reflection* is to deal with
the second sense--showing that this basis is such that it supports religious
truth claims through criteriological investigation. (Ibid., pp. 173,
305fn5). Cf. above, p. 97fn72 on the serious omission in the argument of
the second work.

[6]To cite just two examples: Barth defines the subject matter of dogmatics as "talk about God in the Church" rather than God per se (*Church
Dogmatics*, I.1: 47). Moreover, the truth of such talk is not a matter of
its agreement with God per se but rather its agreement with the "being of
the Church"(Ibid., p. 4). Likewise, Sauter defines the subject matter of
theology as "discourse about God" and considers the existence of such
discourse as self-evident. *Grundlagen*, p. 50.

[7]Cf. *Analogical Imagination*. He characterizes the first part of the
book as a fundamental-theological investigation (85fn31), the heart of
which is the argument about the phenomenon of the classic (xix).

[8]E.g., Thomas Torrance, *Theological Science*, (Oxford: Oxford University
Press, 1969), esp. pp. xiii, 131ff. Actually, Torrance does not wish to
deprive theology of the claim to be a science. Rather, he wants to defend
an understanding of the nature of "science" that is quite different from
the usual model attributed to the natural sciences. He makes "appropriateness to its object" the decisive criterion for determining if a method is
scientific.

[9]G. Sauter, ed., *Wissenschaftstheoretische Kritik der Theologie*,
(Munich: Chr. Kaiser, 1973). N.B., the German word *Wissenschaft* is notor-
iously difficult to translate into English. Its most direct equivalent is
the word "science." However, Germans understand the scope of the
designation to include such inquiries as philosophy, history or sociology,

which are not usually associated with the word "science" in the Anglo-
Saxon realm. Alternative translations would include "scholarship" or
"academic investigation." However, these are rather vague in their meaning.
We have opted for the translation of "Philosophy of Science" for *Wissenschaftstheorie* because of its growing familiarity--cf. Pannenberg's book
in fn 12. However, the reader should bear in mind the scope of the term
thus translated.

[10]Sauter does not claim that all theologians have always proceeded in
this "scientific" manner, only that they can do so. Indeed, the "scientific"
model of theology will become a standard by which Sauter will critique
positional (*Standort*) theologies. (Cf. Sauter, *Grundlagen*, p. 59). There
is present in Sauter, then, a fluctuation between the questions of legitimacy
of theology and legitimacy *in* theology.

[11]Both Sauter's and Pannenberg's discussion of the scientific nature
of theology is framed in terms of the "German" debate whether theology has
a place in the university. Neither considers their work a fundamental
theology per se. However, their central point has a fundamental-theological
focus in terms of the basic intersubjective legitimacy of theological
inquiry.

[12]*Theology and the Philosophy of Science*, (Phil.: Westminster, 1976).

[13]A classic example of this reflection is the Protestant Prolegomenon
to Dogmatics. Cf. Emil Brunner, *The Christian Doctrine of God*, (Phil.:
Westminster, 1950), pp. 3-113; esp. 6-13.

[14]Joest, *Fundamentaltheologie*, p. 9.

[15]The following summary should be read as primarily an attempt to
define this scope, rather than an attempt to provide an innovative organization for these areas of investigation. Such an innovative structure
requires greater development and definition of the various areas of investigation than is presently available.

[16]Cf. Joest, *Fundamentaltheologie*, pp. 143-48. Other subjects that he
mentions are the relation of theology to proclamation, the Church and
society.

[17]It is in light of such questions that Ebeling designates the determination of the type of certainty appropriate to faith as a central
fundamental-theological question. "Fundamentaltheologie," p. 518.

[18]Stirnimann, "Fundamentaltheologie," p. 331.

[19]*Method in Theology*, see p. 4.

[20]*Theology and Philosophy of Science*, see p. 314.

[21]Sauter, *Wissenschaftstheoretische Kritik*, pp. 223-37; and Anton
Grabner-Haider, *Theorie der Theologie als Wissenschaft*, (Munich: Kösel
Verlag, 1974), see p. 123.

[22]John Apczynski, "Integrative Theology: A Polanyian Proposal for
Theological Foundations," TS 40 (1979): 23-43.

[23]Cf. Sauter, *Wissenschaftstheoretische Kritik*, p. 226.

[24]E.g., Söhngen, "Fundamentaltheologie," pp. 453-54; and Joest,
Fundamentaltheologie, p. 9.

[25]Sauter, *Wissenschaftstheoretische Kritik*, p. 13.

[26]A summary of these alternatives is available in Theodore Jennings,
Introduction to Theology, (Phil.: Fortress, 1976), pp. 79-81.

[27]Cf. Joest, *Fundamentaltheologie*, who includes sections on the revelation of God in Jesus Christ, Jesus Christ and the revelation of God in Israel, and the question of general revelation in his chapter on the foundational problematic of theology.

[28]Jennings, *Introduction*, see pp. 1-2.

[29]E.g., Beintker, "Verstehen und Glauben," p. 27; and Stirnimann, "Fundamentaltheologie," p. 331.

[30]Cf. Tillich, *Systematic Theology I*, pp. 34-46.

[31](Missoula, MT: Scholar's Press, 1975).

[32]A good survey of this discussion can be found in *Religious Language and the Problem of Religious Knowledge*, ed. Ronald Santoni, (Bloomington, IN: Indiana University Press, 1968).

[33]Cf. Macquarrie's chapter on "The Language of Theology," which is a constituent part of his philosophical theology. *Principles*, pp. 123-48, esp. 148. See also Grabner-Haider's claim that the main task of fundamental theology is to develop a theory of faith discourse dealing with its assertorial nature and how it means. *Theorie der Theologie*, p. 161.

[34]E.g., Oswald Bayer, *Was ist das: Theologie?* (Stuttgart: Calwer Verlag, 1973), p. 52.

[35]Sauter, *Wissenschaftstheoretische Kritik*, p. 12.

[36]Stirnimann, "Fundamentaltheologie," pp. 353-56. A similar distinction can be found in Koloman Micskey, *Die Axiom-Syntax des evangelischen dogmatischen Denkens*, (Göttingen: Vandenhoeck & Ruprecht, 1976), pp. 136-37.

[37]F. E. Crow, "Foundational Theology," NCE XVII: 235. Lonergan's formulation is given primarily in *Method in Theology*. Page references in this paragraph are to this work.

[38]Cf. Bernard Lonergan, *Insight. A Study of Human Understanding*, (NY: Harper & Row, 1958). Note, however, that this general epistemological reflection is taken up and summarized within the discipline of Foundations in terms of the general categories of transcultural experience (*Method in Theology*, p. 283).

[39]Karl Rahner, "Formal und Fundamentaltheologie," LThK[2] IV: 205-6.

[40]Rahner developed this discipline in conversation with the *Heilsgeschichte* approach to post-Vatican II theology. As such, Darlap's "Fundamentaltheologie des Heilsgeschichte" can be considered a detailed example of formal and fundamental theology in Rahner's sense.

[41]Cf. Karl Rahner, "A Scheme for a Treatise of Dogmatic Theology," *Theological Investigations I*, (NY: Seabury, 1961), pp. 19-37. He distinguishes here between formal theology and fundamental theology, with the latter being a phenomenological investigation of how the categories developed in the former are actually expressed in revelation.

[42]Cf. René Latourelle, "Dismemberment or Renewal of Fundamental Theology?" *Concilium* 46 (1969): 32; and Söhngen, "Fundamentaltheologie," pp. 456-57. An analogous approach is evident in the typically Protestant concern to develop the fundamental doctrines of dogmatics. A good example is Karl Barth's focus on the Word of God as the key to dogmatics in *Church Dogmatics* I.1.

[43]Anders Nygren, *Meaning and Method*, (Phil.: Fortress, 1972).

[44]Cf. Nels F. S. Ferré, *Swedish Contributions to Modern Theology*, (NY: Harper & Row, 1967), p. 68.

[45]For Christianity, Nygren considers the motif to be *agape*.

[46]E.g., Stirnimann, "Fundamentaltheologie," p. 331.

[47]Cf. Monden's ascription of the development of a "true-to-faith" hermeneutic to fundamental theology. *Faith*, p. 12.

[48]*Blessed Rage*, pp. 64-79.

[49]*Naming*, pp. 231-46.

[50]Friedrich Mildenberger, *Theorie der Theologie*, (Stuttgart: Kohlhammer, 1972), p. 45.

[51]Cf. David Tracy, "Theology as Public Discourse," p. 280; idem, *Blessed Rage*, pp. 56fn1, 250fn1; and Gilkey, *Reaping*, p. 369fn3.

[52]Farley, *Ecclesial Reflection*, p. 49.

[53]Anders Jeffner, *Kriterien christlicher Glaubenslehre*, (Uppsala: Upsaliensis Acadamiae, 1977).

[54]That is, particular theological formulations would be investigated to see if they are amenable to the probable results of scientific inquiry. For some theologians the presence of a contradiction between a theological formulation and these scientific criteria would discredit the formulation. For others, the presence of such a contradiction is almost a virtue.

[55]Cf. Sauter, *Grundlagen*, p. 67. Sauter uses the name "metatheory of theology" rather than fundamental theology because he equates the latter with a transcendental analysis of the human like that of Rahner. However, he stresses that his metatheory of theology takes the place of a fundamental theology.

[56](Phil.: Fortress, 1975).

[57]*Die Axiom-Syntax des evangelischen dogmatischen Denkens.* Unfortunately, there are not, to my knowledge, comparable surveys of the criteria and structure of contemporary Catholic theological reflection. Such surveys would be very helpful in furthering the interconfessional discussion by showing similarities and differences between the two confessions at this methodological level.

[58]The components of this axiom-syntax include:
  a) An object with which theology deals
  b) A criterion for dealing with "a"
  c) A central task of dogmatics---measuring "a" by "b"
  d) A medium whereby "b" is obtained
  e) A hermeneutic constant--e.g., common human need
  f) Principles of Rationality
  A_1) Theological Formulation must claim validity
  A_2) Continuity Axiom: dogmatics must embrace predecessors
  A_3) Horizon of Dogmatics--contemporary Zeitgeist

[59]David Tracy's advocacy of a revisionist model of theological judgment is another good example of such reflection. *Blessed Rage*, pp. 43-63.

[60]E.g., Stirnimann, "Fundamentaltheologie," p. 331. Note, however, that some theologians argue against making a theological encyclopedia a part of fundamental theology, for fear of developing a "pantology." Cf. Lang, *Fundamentaltheologie I*, p. 39.

[61]Schubert Ogden, "What is Theology," JR 52 (1972): 34. Indeed, Ogden reserves the specific designation "fundamental theology" for "reflection undertaken within each of the specialties and disciplines

directed toward formulating their respective first principles and thereby
reestablishing communication between them" (35).

[62]*Theology and Philosophy of Science*, pp. 228-440.

[63]*Study of Theology*, p. 157.

[64]Gerhard Ebeling, "Hermeneutische Theologie?" *Wort und Glaube II*,
(Tübingen: J.C.B. Mohr, 1969), p. 113. When Ebeling says that the split
is overcome by a return to the subject matter of theology (*Study*, p. 157),
it must be noted that for him this subject matter is proclamation--both
as the source and goal of theological work. Thus, he is not orienting
the various disciplines to a common object but rather to a common task.

[65]He explicitly denies that *Study of Theology* is such a formulation.
It is instead a collection of reflections on the individual disciplines (8).
The closest model to such an account presently available are the programmatic remarks of Heinrich Ott concerning the hermeneutic arc between
biblical texts and contemporary preaching. Cf. "What is Systematic Theology?"
in *The Later Heidegger and Theology*, eds. J. M. Robinson and J. B. Cobb,
(NY: Harper & Row, 1963), pp. 78-82.

[66]*Method in Theology*.

[67]Cf. Karl Rahner, "Some Critical Reflections on 'Functional Specialties
in Theology'," in *Foundations in Theology*, ed. P. McShane, (University of
Notre Dame Press, 1971), pp. 194-96.

[68]Franz Schupp, *Auf dem Weg zu einer kritischen Theologie*, (Freiburg:
Herder, 1974).

CHAPTER SIX
THE PLACE OF PRAXIS IN
FUNDAMENTAL THEOLOGY

We have reserved for special attention a unique contemporary
approach to fundamental theology: the development of a practical or political fundamental theology.[1] This special attention
is warranted not because this approach presents an entirely
different set of elements for the task of fundamental theology
but rather because this approach presents a unique perspective
on the various elements we have summarized above under the
headings of grounding faith and grounding theology.

It should be noted from the outset that the legitimacy of
this approach is not universally accepted among fundamental
theologians. There is a tendency to assign the concerns which
are characteristic of a practical fundamental theology to some
discipline other than fundamental theology itself. Among the
alternatives mentioned are systematics, moral philosophy and
practical theology.[2] However, we agree with those theologians
who stress the fundamental-theological nature and importance of
these attempts, both in terms of grounding faith and in terms
of grounding theology.[3]

As the title of this chapter suggests, we consider the central contribution of this approach to be a clarification and
defense of the role praxis[4] plays in fundamental-theological
endeavors. We are interested here, then, in showing just what
this role is, through an analysis of these practical fundamental
theologies. We will look first at the methodological implications of these theologies for the various tasks of fundamental
theology as grounding faith and as grounding theology. In a
closing section we will suggest two additional tasks that the
theologies under consideration have shown to be necessary for
a comprehensive fundamental theology.

A. *The Place of Praxis in Grounding Faith*

Johann Baptist Metz's reflections on a practical fundamental theology focus primarily on the role of such a theology in grounding faith.[5] As he puts it: "An essential task of fundamental theology is to defend, justify, or give an account of the authenticity of religion"(7). The most significant contemporary attack on the authenticity of religion, and thus the primary threat against which fundamental theology must defend religion, is idealistic evolutionary systems of thought that claim to be metatheories of theology (7).[6] Normally, such systems of thought operate with an implicit subordination of praxis to theory or idea. The reason that most apologetic attempts to counter the threat of these idealistic systems have failed is that they have uncritically adopted the same subordination into their reflection (50-51). By contrast, a practical fundamental theology would be directly opposed to such a nondialectical subordination of praxis to theory. Instead, it would place great emphasis on the inherent intelligibility of praxis itself (50).

It is in light of this emphasis on the intelligibility of praxis itself that we must understand Metz's description of the task of a practical fundamental theology:

> Its task is to evoke and describe a praxis which will resist all evolutionary attempts at reconstruction and any attempt to do away with religious practice as an independent entity or the religious subject as an authentic aspect in the process of a historical and materialistic dialectical system (7).

At the heart of Metz's practical fundamental theology, then, is a defense of the religious dimension of human existence. It differs from our other examples of such a *demonstratio religiosa*, however, in its emphasis that this defense cannot be executed by mere argument but must be lived--fundamental theology must *evoke* a praxis.[7]

It may be helpful to note one further aspect of Metz's program. He stresses that any defense of the Christian religion must draw on the content of that religion (23). For a practical fundamental theology this means that the praxis it trys to evoke and describe is not just any praxis; rather, it

is an apocalyptic praxis of imitation based on the "dangerous
memory" of the life, teachings and fate of Jesus of Nazareth
(73). That is, the goal of fundamental theology is to evoke in
the Church a praxis in history and society that is based on
the memory of the freedom and hope expressed in the life,
teachings and fate of Jesus, and that is oriented to a future
where this freedom and hope are a socio-political reality (89-90).

B. *The Place of Praxis in Grounding Theology*

As in our previous analysis of the task of grounding theology,
we will distinguish between the attempt to demonstrate the
legitimacy *of* theology and the attempt to insure legitimacy *in*
theology.

1. Praxis and the Legitimacy *of* Theology

Helmut Peukert's discussion of fundamental theology is
essentially an attempt to demonstrate the legitimacy of a practical fundamental theology and, thereby, a practical approach
to theology as a whole.[8] His method for demonstrating this
legitimacy is strongly reminiscent of Pannenberg. That is, he
presents an (ideal[9]) historical overview of the discussion in
the philosophy of science, aimed at showing that his theory of
fundamental theology is its logical and necessary outcome. In
particular, he shows how the aporias of the philosophy of science
have forced it to develop a theory of communicative activity
(76, 222).[10] He also argues that recent fundamental-theological
discussion has moved in this same direction (24). Thus, there
is a convergence between fundamental theology and the philosophy of science in terms of their common concern for
intersubjective communicative activity as the basis of truth (231).

His key argument is that this convergence is not yet complete.
There is a basic problem in the general theory of communicative
activity that can only be solved if it embraces a theological
theory of communicative activity (231). Inherent to a theory
of communicative activity is the ideal of universal communicative solidarity--i.e., the ideal of developing a communicative
activity that is universally available. However, Peukert
argues that the general theory of communicative activity falls
short of such a universal communicative solidarity in one

important regard: it has no solidarity with those in the
past--especially with those in the past who suffered unjustly
(308-9). The solution to this problem lies in the experience
of a communicative, anamnestic solidarity with the innocent
dead that is present and recounted *only* in the Judeo-Christian
tradition (316, 343). As such, an adequate theory of communicative activity must ultimately be developed as a theological
theory of this solidarity (353). For Peukert, fundamental
theology is just such a theory of communicative activity (346).
The fundamental theologian would demonstrate the legitimacy
of theology by formulating a comprehensive theory of communicative activity and showing how theology is based on and
guided by that theory (334fn2).

Even if one doubts the success of Peukert's argument, the
important point is to note his underlying assumption that a
praxis-oriented demonstration of the legitimacy of theology can
serve as a correction and/or supplement to the other demonstra-
tions treated above.

2. Praxis and the Insuring of Legitimacy *in* Theology

Without a doubt, the central concern of political and liberation theologies is to demonstrate the illegitimacy of any
theology that does not take account of social-political reality
in its methods and formulations.[11] Therefore, a practical
fundamental theology must emphasize the task of "elucidating
the basic criteria by which the adequacy of theological methods
and the comprehensiveness of theological constructions can be
evaluated."[12] In particular, political and liberation theologies
have emphasized the necessity of considering socio-political
praxis in determining theology's task, sources and methodological
structure.

a. *Praxis and the Task of Theology*. Gustavo Gutierrez'
definition of the task of theology as "critical reflection on
historical praxis" is typical of the political and liberation
theologians.[13] Usually, this definition is contrasted with
more theoretical definitions typical of existentialist theologians and others.[14]

As Metz points out, the incorporation of the contemporary
emphasis on the eschatological nature of the Christian message
is integral to political theology's reconception of the task
of theology.[15] Political theology can enter into the ambi-
valent processes of historical reality because it realizes
that the truth with which it is concerned is as yet undisclosed
and that its task is to help make present what is currently
available only in hope. That is, the task of theology is not
to show reality as it is but rather to disclose to reality
its future possibilities.[16]

b. *Praxis and the Sources of Theology*. In terms of the
sources of theology, the basic contribution of these theologies
is the defense of the present socio-political situation of the
Church as a source or "text" for theology and not just a hermeneutical horizon within which the meaning of the Christian
faith is to be articulated. That is, theologians must consider
the socio-political situation of the Church when they are trying
to determine what the Christian faith is and not merely when
they are trying to determine the best way to communicate the
Christian faith.[17]

c. *Praxis and the Methods of Theological Judgment*. All in
all, the most characteristic emphasis of political and liberation theologies regarding the place of praxis in fundamental-
theological reflection is on its role in theological
argumentation. This issue has actually become a dividing line
between the (first world) political theologians and the (third
world) liberation theologians. Fiorenza has argued that
political theology tends to move from theory to praxis while
liberation theologies move from praxis to theory.[18] That is,
political theologies take the conceptual message of the gospel
as a starting point and then demand a political hermeneutic
to guide the interpretation of that message.[19] By contrast,
the liberation theologies stress the contemporary socio-
political reality as their starting point.[20] Despite this
difference, both sides agree that the contemporary socio-
political situation must be a criteria of adequate theological
judgments.

C. *Additional Tasks for a Practical Fundamental Theology*

So far we have limited our consideration of the recent formulations of a practical fundamental theology to suggesting
isolated contributions to the various previously established
tasks of fundamental theology. We want now to suggest two
additional tasks that these formulations have urged as incumbent
on any adequate fundamental theology: namely, a theological
pragmatics and a deontology of theology.

Actually, the names and basic definitions of these tasks
were brought into theology through dialogue with the philosophy
of science. The latter had developed an understanding of a
Wissenschaftsethik, which was concerned with locating and
neutralizing the distorting effects of the inclusion of values
in the methodologies of science, and a Pragmatology, which tries
to control the socio-political demands and consequences of
scientific knowledge.[21] The major stimulus for adopting these
categories, however, was the socio-political sensitivity
awakened by political theology.

1. A Theological Pragmatology

A theological pragmatology would consider the practical
implications of the structure and procedures of theological
investigation and teaching.[22] Its focus would be on determining
whether these structures and procedures were conformable to the
task and goal of theological reflection. For example, Metz has
raised serious questions about whether the procedures of contemporary theology--which is normally experienced in libraries
and conferences, where the opinions and counter-opinions of
one's colleagues play a more prominent role than the religious
life and history of suffering of Christian people--prevent it
from adequately fulfilling its role in the Church.[23] The
primary role of such a theological pragmatology would lie in
insuring legitimacy *in* theology. At the same time, the presence
of such considerations in theological reflection would provide
additional warrant for any argument about the legitimacy *of*
theology.

2. A Deontology of Theology

A deontology (or ethic) of theology would consider the ethos of the theologian and the implications of this ethos for the truth of theology.[24] It would ask such questions as: "Who does theology and where, in whose interest and for whom?" The point of such questions is to uncover any ideological bias that may distort theological reflection. For example, an adequate consideration of the Christian understanding of personal possessions can be achieved only in the context of a critical economico-political self-consciousness on the part of the theologian. As Metz argues, it is important that these questions be posed by theology itself and not merely imposed upon it from the outside.[25] Such an inquiry would be fundamental-theological in nature, not merely a part of theological ethics, because it concerns the truth of the theological enterprise as a whole. Again, its focus would be the question of legitimacy *in* theology.

[1]There have been three major attempts in this direction: Francis Fiorenza, "Political Theology as Foundational Theology," *The Catholic Theological Society of America. Proceedings of the 32nd Annual Convention* (1977): 142-77; Johann Baptist Metz, *Faith in History and Society. Towards a Practical Fundamental Theology*, (NY: Seabury, 1980); and Helmut Peukert, *Wissenschaftstheorie - Handlungstheorie - Fundamentaltheologie*, (Düsseldorf: Suhrkamp, 1976).

[2]E.g., Jean-Pierre Torrell, "Questions de Théologie fondamentale," *Revue Thomiste* 79 (1979): 293. See also John Cobb's charge that Tracy has denied the claim of the political theologians to be developing a fundamental theology when he assigns their contribution to practical theology. "Review of Tracy's *Analogical Imagination*," RelStR 7 (1981): 282.

[3]E.g., Claude Geffré, *A New Age in Theology*, (NY: Paulist, 1974), p. 94; and Johann Baptist Metz, "Political Theology," EnTh, p. 1239.

[4]The category "praxis" is a specialized term developed by Marxists and critical theorists to overcome the split between supposedly rational "reflection" and arational "activity." It might best be defined as purposeful or meaningful human activity as expressed in a particular historical, socio-political environment. Accordingly, a "practical" fundamental theology is one which devotes a central role in its analyses to such "praxis."

[5]*Faith*. Page references in next four paragraphs are to this work.

[6]Metz understands these systems to be heirs of the Enlightenment (27). Thus, the development of his practical fundamental theology is one of the

expressions of the theological enlightenment about the Enlightenment that
was noted to be characteristic of the contemporary discussion. Cf., above,
p. 50.

[7]Note, in this regard, that Fiorenza has spoken approvingly of the
understanding of fundamental theology that focuses on the actual process
of conversion. He assigns to his foundational theology the task of reflecting on "the total praxis of religious conversion and flowing from religious
conversion." "Political Theology," p. 143.

[8]Peukert, *Wissenschaftstheorie*. A good English summary of Peukert is
available in Rudolf J. Siebert, "Peukert's Critical Theology," *The Ecumenist*
16 (1977): 52-58, 78-80. Since Peukert never calls his work a *practical*
fundamental theology, our treatment of him here requires justification.
We would note two points. First, Peukert formulates his view as a corollary
of the theory of communicative activity (*Handeln*) developed by Jürgen
Habermas. This theory was developed specifically to overcome the split
between praxis and theory that Metz considers the arch nemesis of a practical
fundamental theology. Second, Peukert was a student of Metz and Metz refers
to his work as a continuation of the basic intentions of political theology
(*Faith*, p. 12fn5).

[9]Peukert has been charged with selectively presenting this history in
such a way that it leads to his point. Cf. Karl-Fritz Daiber's review of
his book in EvTh 38 (1978): 448-49.

[10]A theory of communicative activity is a particular position regarding
the epistemological question of what constitutes "rationality" or truth. It
was develped as an alternative to such theories as the logical positivists,
empiricists and intuitionists. Taking its lead from Wittgenstein's emphasis
that meaning arises within a given context and J. L. Austin's analysis of
the interaction of speech and activity in expressing meaning, such a theory
argues that "rationality" is a function of communicative interaction. The
test of truth is not comparison of "discourse" with some extra-linguistic
reality but rather conformity with the grammatical rules of successful
interpersonal communicative activity. Cf. Jürgen Habermas, *Knowledge and
Human Interests*, (Boston: Beacon, 1972), p. 192.

[11]Metz, "Political Theology," p. 1239.

[12]Fiorenza, "Political Theology," p. 143.

[13]Gutierrez, *A Theology of Liberation*, (Maryknoll, NY: Orbis, 1973),
p. 10.

[14]Cf. Dorothee Sölle, *Political Theology*, (Phil.: Fortress, 1974),
p. 60.

[15]Metz, "Political Theology," p. 1239.

[16]Cf. Jürgen Moltmann, *Theology of Hope*, (NY: Harper & Row, 1967),
pp. 32-36.

[17]Cf. J. Andrew Kirk, *Liberation Theology*, (Atlanta, GA: John Knox,
1979), pp. 36-37.

[18]Fiorenza, "Political Theology," pp. 167-71.

[19]Cf. Jürgen Moltmann, "Toward a Political Hermeneutic of the Gospel,"
in *Religion, Revolution and the Future*, (NY: Scribner's, 1969), pp. 83-107.

[20]Cf. Gutierrez, *Liberation*, p. 269. A detailed example of the latter
alternative is found in Juan Segundo, *The Liberation of Theology*, (Maryknoll,
NY: Orbis, 1976), p. 9: "Firstly, there is our way of experiencing reality,
which leads us to ideological suspicion. Secondly, there is the application

of our ideological suspicion to the whole ideological superstructure general and to theology in particular. Thirdly, there comes a new wa experiencing theological reality that leads us to exegetical suspicion, that is, to the suspicion that the prevailing interpretations of the Bible have not taken important pieces of data into account. Fourthly, we have our new hermeneutic, that is, our new way of interpreting the fountainhead of our faith with the new aspects at our disposal."

[21]Cf. Sauter, *Wissenschaftstheoretische Kritik*, pp. 13, 75-143.

[22]Stirnimann, "Fundamentaltheologie," p. 357.

[23]Metz, *Faith*, p. 137.

[24]Stirnimann, "Fundamentaltheologie," p. 357.

[25]Metz, *Faith*, pp. 58-59.

PART THREE

PROPOSAL FOR AN ECUMENICAL
FUNDAMENTAL THEOLOGY

INTRODUCTION

The final task of this essay is a constructive one. So far we have surveyed the history of the discipline of fundamental theology and gained an overview of the variety of contemporary understandings of its task and scope. In both cases, we devoted particular attention to the interconfessional aspects of the discussion. Through this investigation we have obtained a taxonomy of the diversity of tasks that have been assigned to this discipline, both interconfessionally and intraconfessionally. We have, thereby, become aware of the difficulties involved in talking about *an* ecumenical fundamental theology.

Nonetheless, it is precisely the formulation of a proposal for such *an* ecumenical fundamental theology that will occupy us in this final section of our investigation. This proposal will not be simply an amalgamation of the various elements located in our typological overview. Such an amalgamation is impossible because some of these elements are exclusive of each other. Moreover, such an approach would lack the central focus necessary to talk of fundamental theology per se rather than merely a group of somewhat related activities. On the other hand, the proposal must be developed in light of and take a stance towards the various activities that have been assigned to a fundamental theology. In particular, it must deal with the central tasks of grounding faith and grounding theology. Are both of these integral to fundamental theology? If so, then in what manner and how are they to be related?

Answers to these questions will have implications for the "ecumenical" nature of our proposed understanding of fundamental theology. As throughout this essay, we are limiting our proposal to questions of the basic task and scope of fundamental theology. Thus, when we designate this an "ecumenical fundamental theology," we mean that the understanding of its task and scope is such that the central concerns of the various

133

confessions can find expression within it. In particular,
while we have seen that it is no longer accurate to see
"grounding faith" as exclusively the Catholic understanding of
the task of fundamental theology and "grounding theology" as
exclusively the Protestant understanding, a truly ecumenical
understanding of the discipline must come to terms with both
of these tasks.

CHAPTER SEVEN
THE TASK AND SCOPE OF
FUNDAMENTAL THEOLOGY

As a starting point for discussing our proposal for an
ecumenical fundamental theology we would advance the following
brief definition:

> Fundamental theology is the moment of theological inquiry charged
> with critical reflection on the Christian faith, as this faith is
> articulated in Christian theology, with the goal of insuring the
> legitimacy of this theological exposition of Christian faith.

Several aspects of this definition deserve special attention.
First, we are assuming an understanding of faith which refuses
to separate unduly between faith itself and the conceptual
theological explications of faith. While any particular theological explication will suffer limitations and must be tested
for legitimacy, it is misleading to emphasize a supposed
"pre-conceptual" nature of faith, as if all explications were
imposed and secondary. At the core of Christian faith is a
basic understanding of the relationship of God and humanity
in the world. Theology explicates this understanding. Thus,
one cannot ground Christian faith without entering into considerations of Christian theology, and vice versa.

Second, the task of fundamental theology is defined as
critical reflection on the theological exposition of Christian
faith. That is, fundamental theology is not commissioned to
create theological formulations but rather to reflect critically
on already existing formulations. Or again, fundamental theology
is not concerned with the defense of theological formulations
but rather with the inquiry into their legitimacy.

Third, our choice of the word "legitimacy" is intentional,
in light of discussions about the verification or truth of
theological statements. Legitimacy refers to a state of "con-
forming to recognized principles or accepted rules and standards."[1]

In choosing to talk of the "legitimacy" of theological formulations we are opting for a consensus model of truth. However,
it is a critical consensus model. In particular, we are drawing
on many of the suggestions of Jürgen Habermas's theory of
communicative competence.[2] As Habermas argues, an adequate
understanding of a consensus model of truth does not surrender
to every prevailing consensus. Rather, it tests the competence
of the communicative activity within which the consensus arose.
An adequate consensus is one which was developed in a critical
and competent communicative dialogue. This is important for
our discussion because when we argue, for example, that theological formulations must be tested for legitimacy in light of
general human inquiry, we do not mean that theologians simply
accept particular philosophical, psychological, or other theories
as norms. Rather, it is often necessary for theologians to
enter into a critical analysis of the adequacy of such theories.[3]

     Fourth, there are two basic areas in which the legitimacy of
theological formulations come into question: in regard to
general human inquiry and in regard to their unique subject
matter. Thus, a legitimate theological formulation is one
whose sources, language, methods of formulation and basic
claims can be shown to be appropriate and/or meaningful in terms
of the critically accepted standards of general human inquiry
and the critically determined subject matter of specifically
theological inquiry.

     Finally, the goal of the fundamental theologian's critical
reflection on the formulations of Christian theology is to
ground theology--in the sense of insuring that theology proceeds
in a critically validated manner--and, thereby, to ground
Christian faith by promoting a critical self-understanding of
Christian faith among believers.

     The remainder of this chapter will be devoted to clarifying
and defending our understanding of fundamental theology through
a consideration of four central issues regarding the task and
scope of the discipline: a) the role of fundamental theology
in grounding faith, b) the role of fundamental theology in
grounding theology, c) the interconnection of grounding faith
and grounding theology, and d) the relationship of fundamental
theology to extratheological inquiry. We will then consider

two further subsidiary issues: e) practical considerations
related to this understanding of fundamental theology, and
f) the appropriateness of the name "fundamental theology" for
the task described.

A. *Fundamental Theology and the Grounding of Faith*

The first step in further clarifying our understanding of
fundamental theology is to define its role in grounding faith.
The essential question in this connection is the relation of
fundamental theology to apologetics.

Fundamental theology originally developed in close correlation with apologetic activities. The earliest Protestant usages
of the term referred to a defense of the sources of Christian
theology. Likewise, the typical Catholic discipline of fundamental theology was devoted to an argumentative defense of the
possibility and need for a divine revelation, along with
arguments for the validity of the Christian claim to be that
revelation and the Catholic claim to mediate that revelation.
However, discussions concerning that task and method of fundamental theology have been characterized since the beginning by
a tension between an approach that aims at an argumentative
apologetic for Christian faith (e.g., Kleuker, neo-Scholasticism)
and an approach that aims at a phenomenological/hermeneutic
explication of Christian faith (e.g., Schleiermacher, Blondel,
Vatican II). This tension is not incidental but rather a
direct result of trying to embrace two distinct--albeit
related--tasks under one heading.

There has been an increasing awareness of the distinct
nature of these tasks in recent fundamental-theological discussion. For example, while the terms "apologetics" and
"fundamental theology" were essentially interchangeable in
Catholic theology during the neo-Scholastic period, the recent,
more phenomenological/hermeneutic Catholic fundamental theologians have argued for the preference of the term "fundamental
theology" over "apologetics." Their reason for doing so was
that "fundamental theology" connoted a positive explicative
activity, while "apologetics" connoted a defensive argumentative activity.[4] This distinction raises the question of the

relationship of such a fundamental theology and such an
apologetics.

There have been two responses to this question. First,
there are those who see fundamental theology as incorporating
or usurping the apologetic enterprise. That is, fundamental
theology becomes the contemporary form of apologetics.[5] Whereas
the negative argumentative form may have been acceptable in a
previous setting, the most appropriate method of grounding
faith in the contemporary setting is to show its positive meaning and value for human life by explicating its nature and
structures.[6] The second response is that fundamental theology
and apologetics need to be viewed as two distinct, equally
legitimate, contemporary theological activities.[7] Apologetics
is then construed as theological reflection on Christian faith
that is aimed primarily at defending or recommending[8] that
faith to nonbelievers. By contrast, fundamental theology is
construed as reflection on Christian faith that is aimed at
promoting a critical self-understanding of the essential nature
and structures of that faith. While these two disciplines are
distinct, they are not totally separate since fundamental
theology provides the basis for apologetic argumentation.

The second response is the most appropriate to the subject
matter (*Sache*) under consideration and provides the most helpful perspective for developing an ecumenical fundamental
theology.[9] Two considerations lend support to this view.

First, any proof or defense presupposes some understanding
or insight into that which is being proven or defended.[10] Moreover, it presupposes an understanding developed in light of the
criticisms or alternative positions that are to be the focus of
the proof or defense. That is, in order to adequately defend
the Christian faith against a particular criticism, one must
first engage in a critical clarification of the essential
claims of the Christian faith that are in question so that the
real issues can be addressed.

The second consideration is closely related to the first.
Recent discussion about "grounding faith" has demonstrated that
the development of a critical self-understanding among believers
is as integral to this task as the argument for faith aimed at
nonbelievers.[11] It thereby becomes possible to talk of a

fundamental-theological approach to grounding faith--i.e., the
promotion of a critical self-understanding of faith--that is
distinct from the apologetic approach of recommending or
defending faith. In light of the consideration that proof rests
on understanding, we would argue that this fundamental-theological
task of promoting a critical self-understanding of faith is
foundational to the apologetic task of recommending or defending
faith.[12]

In light of these considerations we would ascribe to fundamental theology the task of promoting a critical self-understanding of Christian faith. The stimulus for developing such a
critical self-understanding typically comes from the confrontation with questions about the generally held understanding of
Christian faith. These questions have frequently come from
"outside" of faith but are increasingly being raised by Christ-
ians themselves. While such questions can concern any aspect
of Christian faith, they are by and large reducible to questions
about the basic world view of that faith--i.e., what does
Christian faith imply about the relationship of God and humanity
in the world? For example, questions might be raised about
whether certain understandings of "God" are integral to Christian
faith or, alternatively, whether Christian faith has an inherent
deprecation of the "world." The fundamental theologian is
charged with promoting a critical reexamination of the present
understanding of the world view of Christian faith in light of
such questions.[13] Of course, the result of such an examination might be to highlight the difference between Christian
faith and its critics, rather than to overcome this difference.
The benefit of fundamental-theological reflection remains,
however, because the awareness of this difference is now a
self-critical awareness. In short, such reflection would
ground Christian faith in the sense that believers would be
made aware of the essential claims of Christian faith and
would be shown that these claims have theological warrant.

While fundamental theology is assigned the task of critically
clarifying the world view of Christian faith in light of possible questions regarding that world view, apologetics is
assigned the task of promoting the acceptance of that world
view among nonbelievers by portraying its meaning and value

and by defending it against criticism. Significantly, apologists operate under the constraint that they must state their
case using arguments that the critics of faith would consider
admissible (i.e., they cannot appeal to faith as a self-evident
warrant[14]).

What then is the relationship between apologetics and fundamental theology? We have already argued that fundamental
theology can ground faith in a manner that is distinct from
apologetics, namely, the promotion of a critical self-understanding of Christian faith among believers. We want now to
add that fundamental theology also grounds the apologetic
enterprise in the sense that it provides the apologist with a
critical self-understanding of that which she or he is to
recommend or defend.

We can gain a better understanding of the relationship
between fundamental theology and apologetics, as well as further
insight into their differences, by considering the example of
their unique roles in responding to the recurrent modern
accusation that the Christian faith demeans secular human life.
The initial theological response to such a charge would be (and
has been) an apologetic one--namely, an argument that, on the
contrary, the Christian faith can and has served to fulfill
human life in all its aspects. At a surface level this argument
could be advanced by such means as the claim that the contemporary Western understanding of individual human worth is itself
a by-product of the Christian tradition. As the debate deepens,
however, it may become necessary to undertake the fundamental-
theological task of reconsidering just what views of the Divine,
humanity and the world are constitutive of the Christian world
view after all. The development of such a critical self-
understanding of the world view of Christian faith is a
continuous undertaking. Historically, it was the persistent
accusation about the demeaning nature of Christian faith for
secular life that prompted theologians like Bonhoeffer to engage
in fundamental-theological reconceptions of the place of the
"religious" and the "secular" in Christian faith.[15] That is,
the recurrent accusations to which the apologists were trying
to respond prompted renewed fundamental-theological reflection

which, in turn, provided apologetics with a new understanding
of the Christian world view itself to recommend.

This example suggests the importance of viewing fundamental
theology and apologetics as distinct theological tasks. Such
a distinction clarifies and preserves the contructive role of
dialogue with the critics of Christian faith.   Christian
apologists have too often approached their task as if the "truth"
of faith was already available in a definitive explication, and
as if their only task was to defend this explication. Fundamental theology, as we are defining it, is concerned with the
necessary and logically prior task of reappraising the present
explication of Christian faith in light of the critical questions, so that the real claims of Christian faith can be
distinguished from inadequate formulations of these claims.   In
light of such clarification a more profitable apologetic dialogue
with the critics of faith could take place.

At the same time, one must not *unduly* separate apologetics
and fundamental theology since one of the functions of fundamental theology is to provide a basis for apologetics. Perhaps
the best solution is to refer to them as distinct "moments" in
the larger theological enterprise. Such a solution would help
guard against the misunderstanding that our distinction
between fundamental theology and apologetics entails a rigid
separation of fundamental-theological and apologetic reflection
in constructive theological formulations. Indeed, many
effective theological works have been an intentional mixture
of these two.[16] Practical didactic considerations will often
warrant such interpenetrations of the different moments of
theological reflection. Nonetheless, it is important to
achieve a clarity about the distinct moments of this larger
enterprise when one is engaged in encyclopedic reflection--and
all reflection on the task and scope of a particular discipline
is encyclopedic reflection.

This point brings us to our last consideration in this
section: Just how does our understanding of the role of fundamental theology in grounding faith relate to the various
positions summarized in chapter four of this essay? Put suc-
cinctly, we would accept the central concerns of each of the
three *demonstrationes* but would distinguish between apologetic

and fundamental-theological formulations of these concerns.
For example, it is a valid task of fundamental theology to seek
a critical understanding of the implications of Christian faith
regarding the nature of the human and the Divine. However,
when one moves from such an inner-faith ontological clarification (e.g., Hart) to a purportedly rational argument for a
universal religious apriori (e.g., Rahner), one has moved from
fundamental-theological reflection to apologetics. Again, there
can be a valid use of correlation in fundamental theology to
deepen the understanding of the uniquely Christian claims about
reality and human existence. However, when one moves from
using correlation to develop a contemporary understanding of
the Christian world view (e.g., Biser) to an argument that
Christian faith is the most adequate fulfillment and representation of "secular faith" (Tracy), one has again left the realm
of fundamental theology for that of apologetics. Finally, it
is helpful to emphasize the necessary social, ecclesial dimen-
sions of the Christian faith. However, all three examples of
this approach which we considered in chapter four focused on
this topic more in terms of the apologetic task of defending
Christian faith than in terms of the fundamental-theological
task of facilitating a better self-understanding of that faith.

   This proposal also embraces the basic issues involved in
the emphasis on conversion in fundamental theology and in
Rahner's foundational course. Regarding the former, one must
again distinguish between considerations of the nature and role
of conversion that aim at a better understanding of the complexity of Christian faith and its relationship to human life and
those that try to show that Christian conversion is appropiate,
desirable, or necessary for human life. Likewise, Rahner's
point about the didactic need to accept the provisional status
of fundamental-theological reflection is valid, even if his own
definition of the task of fundamental theology is more apologetic than our own. Fundamental theologians must be willing
to give provisional presentations of the critically appraised
world view of Christian faith, even though they know that
these presentations are subject to improvement or change.

B. *Fundamental Theology and the Grounding of Theology*

So far we have been clarifying the way in which fundamental
theology grounds Christian faith. Our task now is to explain
how fundamental theology grounds theology. We will develop
this explanation by taking a stance on several issues that have
proven to be significant in discussions about fundamental
theology's role in grounding theology.

1) In the contemporary setting, one of the first tasks of
a discipline charged with grounding theology is the critical
development and assessment of the methods used in theological
investigation and argumentation. Does such a task belong to
fundamental theology? The answer to this question depends upon
one's understanding of what is involved in critically assessing
such methods. It is possible to limit one's assessment to such
questions as the "testability" of the methods of investigation
and the logical consistency of the methods of argumentation.
While these questions are important, they have not yet reached
a truly fundamental-theological level. That is, they have not
reflected on the adequacy of these methods from a strictly
theological perspective. A fundamental-theological consideration of the methods of theology *is* interested in determining if
these methods are consonant with general human inquiry. However,
it is *also*, and most characteristically interested in determining
if these methods are consonant with the theological subject
matter with which they are to deal. It is only when the second
question is asked that a consideration of the methods of theology transcends the level of technique and becomes a fundamental
theological consideration. Thus, not every consideration of
theological method is a fundamental-theological consideration.
However, we would argue that considerations of theological
method that fail to penetrate to the fundamental-theological
level of questioning are ultimately inadequate.

2) The counterpoint to the fact that not every consideration of theological methods is a fundamental-theological
consideration is that fundamental theology itself cannot be
reduced to questions of theological method.[17] If a central
focus of a fundamental-theological investigation of theology's
methods is the question of whether these methods are

appropriate to the subject matter of theology, then a crucial
task of fundamental theology is to develop a critical self-
understanding of that subject matter. We have argued earlier
that the essential subject matter of theology can best be
defined as an understanding of the relationship of God and the
human in the world. That is, the essential subject matter of
theology is the world view implicit in Christian faith. The
fundamental-theological task of promoting a critical self-
understanding of the subject matter of theology would involve
a critical consideration of this world view.[18]

3) The task just described may appear to belong to dogmatic
or systematic theology rather than fundamental theology. Therefore, the next task we must undertake is to clarify the
distinction between fundamental theology and doctrinal theology.
We will develop this clarification by first defining doctrinal
theology and then considering fundamental theology's relationship to the former.

To understand doctrinal theology[19] one must first understand
the role of doctrine in the life of the Christian community.[20]
Doctrine is not primary religious discourse. That is, it is
not an immediate expression of a religious community on the
order of liturgy, prayer, or proclamation. Rather, it is
second-order disourse that aims at giving an intelligible
account of such primary religious discourse. As one moves from
doctrine per se to doctrinal theology, a further point emerges.
Doctrinal theology is not concerned merely to provide a collection of intelligible doctrinal explications of the primary
religious discourse of a community. Rather, it has a corrective
and normative function over-against the community's primary
discourse. Two aspects of this corrective function are particularly important. First, one of the principal tasks of
doctrinal theology is to investigate the implications of the
various expressions of the community for each other and thereby
develop an integrated understanding of the world view of the
community. Such an investigation will often find it necessary
to propose corrections to certain practices and expressions of
the community in light of other practices and expressions, all
in the interest of an integrated self-understanding. Second,
doctrinal theology not only investigates the interrelationships

of the various contemporary expressions of a community, it also
engages in a normative investigation of the correlation of
these contemporary expressions with past expressions, particularly those which the community has designated as the norm for
faith and practice. In both corrective activities the focus
is on clarifying and purifying the belief and practice of the
community *for the community*, not for those outside the
community.

In brief, Christian doctrinal theology has the task of
developing an intelligible and integrated account of the primary religious expressions of the Christian community and
engaging in normative criticism of those expressions in light
of this account and the established norms of the community.
In its most concise form, such an integrated account could be
called a presentation of the self-understood world view of the
community.

Whereas doctrinal theology is assigned the task of developing
an integrated account of the world view of the Christian community, fundamental theology is assigned the task of reflection
on this world view in light of the critical questions raised
about it.

Perhaps the best way to further clarify this relationship
is to reflect on the task of Christian theology as a whole.
Because of its intrinsic missionary emphasis, Christian theology has always occupied a bipolar position between the
Christian community and the "world." It has had to carry on
its work in a way that was responsible to the Christian community and yet, at the same time, intelligible and challenging
to the "world." Doctrinal theology and apologetics (in both
its positive and negative modes) represent the "moments" of
theological reflection that correspond to the bipolar position
of theology. Doctrinal theology focuses on integrating, clarifying and normatively correcting the faith and practice of the
Christian community. Apologetics, on the other hand, aims at
commending the Christian message to the "world" in terms the
"world" will understand and at defending this message against
external critique.

What is the place of fundamental theology in this larger
perspective? It is a meta-reflective moment of theological

inquiry aimed at critically analyzing the world view of Christian faith as formulated in doctrinal theology and defended in
apologetic theology. On the one hand, it critically assesses
the formulations of this world view to determine if their
methods of formulation, sources, language, etc., are legitimate
and/or adequate to the Christian faith. On the other hand, it
reflects on these formulations of the world view of Christian
faith in light of the critical questions raised about them to
determine what claims are essential to this world view and what
claims are instead expressions of the inadequacy or inappro-
priateness of the formulations.

The goal of such fundamental-theological reflection is not
to replace either doctrinal theology or apologetics. Rather,
it is to facilitate the legitimate functioning of both. On
the side of doctrinal theology, the clarity gained about the
legitimate and essential elements of the world view of Christian
faith would aid in its task of integrating and correcting the
life and practice of the Christian community.[21] On the side
of apologetics, the insight into the essential claims of
Christian faith would aid the location of the real issues in
the dialogue with the critics of faith and, thereby, aid in
presenting a more effective apology for faith.

It might be objected that this analysis of the relationship
of fundamental theology to doctrinal theology and apologetics
portrays the latter two as being inherently uncritical. Two
points can be made in response. First, it is precisely the
task of the fundamental-theological moment of reflection to
insure that the doctrinal and apologetic moments do *not* function uncritically. Second, a matter-of-fact acceptance of the
critical element in doctrinal or apologetic theology is more
likely to lead to a disregard of this element than is an isolation of this critical moment for special attention. As stated
earlier, our emphasis on the need to gain clarity about the
distinct moments of the larger theological enterprise should
not be misconstrued as an argument to isolate these moments
from one another.

Further clarity on the distinction between fundamental
theology and doctrinal theology may be gained by returning to
our example of the theological response to the accusation that

Christian faith demeans secular human life. We noted previously
that the task of providing an adequate apologetic response to
this accusation was dependent upon the fundamental-theological
task of gaining a critical self-understanding of what views of
the Divine, humanity and the world are constitutive of Christian
faith after all. What role does doctrinal theology play in such
an endeavor? Put briefly, fundamental theologians would begin
with the present doctrinal formulations of the Christian world
view. They would analyze these formulations in light of the
contemporary accusation to determine what really is implied by
this understanding of Christian faith. Integral to this analysis would be the investigation of whether the methods, language,
etc., of the present formulations are such that they can be
judged to be appropriate and/or adequate expressions of the
Christian faith. One may find that significant data was left
unconsidered or misconstrued by these formulations, and
therefore they are misleading. For example, Bonhoeffer has
argued that the ultimate implication of Paul's rejection of
circumcision as a condition of justification is the rejection
of "religion" as a condition of salvation.[22] In light of such
a critical reflection, fundamental theologians would articulate
what they believe to be the essential claims of Christian faith
regarding the relation of the "religious" and the "secular."
However, the theological response to this accusation does not
end here. Rather, it is now incumbent upon doctrinal theologians to incorporate this critically reevaluated understanding
of the world view of Christian faith into their own reflections
and to work out the numerous implications of this understanding
for the life and practice of the Christian community. Much of
the work of the "theologians of secularity" demonstrates this
process.[23]

   To summarize the distinction: when one is engaged in trying
to understand the primary religious expressions of the Christian
community, one is engaged in doctrinal theology. Even when one
engages in an investigation of the implications of the various
expressions of the community with the goal of developing an
integrated world view of the community, one is still engaged
in doctrinal theology. However, when one begins to reflect on
the legitimacy of the doctrinal formulations expressing this

world view--both in terms of their appropriateness and/or
adequacy in expressing Christian faith and in terms of their
appropriateness and/or significance for general human inquiry--
one has moved into the realm of fundamental theology. Finally,
when one returns to consider the implications for the life
and practice of the Christian community of any changes in the
understanding of the world view of Christian faith mandated
by the fundamental-theological investigation, one has returned
to the realm of doctrinal theology.

Thus, whereas doctrinal theology's task starts with a consideration of the various primary religious expressions of the
Christian community and aims at an integrative presentation of
the world view of Christian faith, fundamental theology starts
with this world view as presented in doctrinal theology and
aims at a critical understanding of it in light of the critical
questions raised about it. In short, fundamental theology is
related to doctrinal theology as a type of meta-reflection on
the latter with the aim of insuring legitimacy in doctrinal
formulations.

4) This understanding of the relationship of doctrinal
theology and fundamental theology provides the background for
responding to a recent attempt by Otto Pesch to reduce fundamental theology to a pedagogical introduction to dogmatics.[24]
Pesch developed his understanding of fundamental theology in
response to Heinrich Stirnimann's definition of fundamental
theology as an introductory discipline which attempts to articulate the subject of theological assertions.[25] Pesch's
problem with this understanding is that he considers it impossible to introduce something without going through its contents
(465). As such, all fundamental theology would be doing is
giving a preliminary overview of dogmatics. It could be
described as "grounding" theology only in a pedagogical sense--
that is, as a first step of reflection in the terms of Rahner's
foundational course (463). In this light, Pesch uses the
contemporary rapprochment between fundamental theology and
dogmatics to argue that there is no need for fundamental theology as a separate discipline. Its present existence as an
introductory discipline is, at best, a result of the practical
difficulties of teaching theology (468).

The problem with which Pesch is struggling comes as a direct result of the closer correlation of fundamental theology and doctrinal theology. We have seen that fundamental theology does indeed enter into a consideration of the "content" of doctrinal theology. However, it is extremely misleading to talk of fundamental theology as merely a pedagogical introduction to doctrinal theology, for this suggests that the type of consideration this "content" receives is the same in both disciplines. There are at least four points that need to be made against a view of fundamental theology as a pedagogical introduction to doctrinal theology.

a) One of the common ways of conceiving of fundamental theology as an introduction to doctrinal theology is to assign to it the task of developing the categories of doctrinal theology. We treated three variations of such a view in our typology, as represented by Lonergan, Rahner and Nygren. The problem with such a conception is that it suggests that fundamental theology formulates theological concepts and then doctrinal theology uses them. On the contrary, theological concepts arise in the course of Christian life and doctrinal reflection on that life. Fundamental theology finds these concepts as a "given" and is charged with the responsibility of reflecting on their legitimacy.

b) Of course, one could understand the task of fundamental theology as presenting a general overview of the basic concepts of theology without assuming that fundamental theology develops these concepts. Rather than creating these concepts, fundamental theology would "distill" them. Such would appear to be the view of Pesch. The problem with this view is that it misconstrues the purpose of fundamental-theological reflection on the theological concepts developed in doctrinal theology. Fundamental theology does *not* aim at "distilling" theological concepts into appropriate pedagogical form for an introductory course. Rather, it engages in a critical analysis of these concepts with the goal of bringing clarity and heightened legitimacy to their use in doctrinal theology. The fact that this critical analysis often takes the form of a focused analysis of the concepts determined to be most central to Christian faith should not be confused with an attempt to summarize faith.

c) The emphasis on fundamental theology's task of promoting legitimacy in theological reflection suggests another problem with the conception of fundamental theology as a pedagogical introduction to doctrinal theology. The concern to promote legitimacy in theological reflection makes it necessary for the fundamental theologian to devote direct attention to several issues that are not a primary focus of doctrinal theology. For example, we have seen that questions of theological method play a significant role in fundamental-theological reflection. One of the ways fundamental theology tests the legitimacy of the formulations of doctrinal theology is to reflect on the adequacy and appropriateness of the methods used in constructing these formulations. Other considerations that our typological investigation showed to be constitutive of the fundamental-theological task of insuring legitimacy *in* theology relate to 1) the task or goal of theology, 2) the sources of theology, 3) the language of theology, and 4) the unity of theology. Obviously, such considerations are not totally absent from doctrinal theology. Indeed, it is fundamental theology's task to insure they are not! However, these considerations are not a primary focus of doctrinal reflection as they are in fundamental theology. A discipline with a focus so distinct from that of doctrinal theology would be a poor pedagogical introduction to the "content" of the latter.[26]

d) Finally, we would resist the move to treat fundamental theology as primarily a pedagogical introduction to doctrinal theology because its concern for legitimacy in theology is related to the theological enterprise as a whole, not just doctrinal theology.[27] We noted earlier that fundamental theology plays an important role in facilitating and grounding apologetics. Another important part of the fundamental-theological task of insuring legitimacy in theological reflection is the clarification of the theological implications of such disciplines as biblical studies, church history, ethics or pastoral theology.[28] In particular, the fundamental theologian must undertake an inquiry into the unity of these diverse fields and show how each of these areas contributes to and draws from the special work of doctrinal theology.

In light of these various considerations we would prefer
to designate the task of fundamental theology as "grounding
theology" rather than "providing a pedagogical introduction
to doctrinal theology." The way it "grounds" theology is by
assuring that theology proceeds in a legitimate manner.

5) All that has been said so far leads us to side with
those who argue that fundamental theology should be considered
a separate "moment" (or discipline) in the larger theological
enterprise. This is desirable not merely because the scope of
the questions treated in a fundamental theology has grown so
significantly[29] but because the work of theology itself has
pressed for special consideration of the question of its legitimacy.[30] In other words, we consider the contemporary flood
of fundamental-theological reflection to be an expression of
a self-imposed theological task and not merely a response to
the external demands of the sciences and other religions and
ideologies.[31]

6) If fundamental theology should be considered as a
separate moment of theological reflection, then the last issue
we must address is: What is the encyclopedic relationship of
fundamental theology to the other moments of theological
reflection? There have been two answers to this question:
either fundamental theology stands at the beginning of theological reflection (or at least prior to doctrinal theology
as theology proper) or it stands at the end. We will develop
our understanding in relation to these alternatives.

There are at least three different understandings of fundamental theology as preceding theology proper. The most
ambitious such conception sees fundamental theology as a
foundational science that formulates a general understanding
of reality as a whole on the basis of which subsequent theological reflection can take place. A clear representative of
such an approach is Helmut Peukert.[32] He sees fundamental
theology as developing a critical theory of communicative
activity and the reality of God which is experienced in this
activity.[33] Theology proper would then be based on and guided
by this theory. Two comments are in order relative to this
view. First, it is difficult to see how such an abstract
theory can adequately or effectively ground the practical

discipline of theology. Second, while fundamental theology
might well reflect on the implications of something like a
theory of communicative activity for theology or suggest
correctives to such a theory on the basis of theology, we
would not regard the *construction* of such a theory as the primary task of fundamental theology. Fundamental theology's
concern with the world view of Christian faith is not aimed
at building a theoretical basis for subsequent theology but
rather at pursuing a meta-theological inquiry into the legitimacy of existing theological reflection.

A second way of construing fundamental theology as preceding
theology proper is to claim that it establishes a prior horizon
within which the various theological formulations can be understood and judged.[34] This view is normally tied to a conception
of fundamental theology as developing the concepts for the rest
of theology. We have already suggested the problem with such
a conception. Essentially, it is that we understand fundamental theology to reflect on the legitimacy of concepts
already promulgated in theological inquiry and not to create
concepts which can then be embraced in theological formulations.

A final way of construing fundamental theology as preceding
theology proper is based on an understanding of fundamental
theology as apologetic in nature. It argues that fundamental
theology precedes theology in the sense that it "makes room"
for theological reflection to take place.[35] By defending the
basic concepts, sources and methods of theology, we can clear
the way for actual theology to commence. Many of those whom
we treated in our typology under the heading "Demonstrating
the Legitimacy *of* Theology" would fit this view. There are
two difficulties with this view. First, fundamental theology
is not concerned with defending the methods or sources of
theology but rather with clarifying and critiquing them. The
defense of appropriately critical methods is an apologetic
task. Second, even if this defense were a fundamental-theological task, it is misleading to speak of such a defense as
"preceding" theology per se because such a defense would have
to refer to actual theological reflection to substantiate its
claim that theological methods are critically appropriated.

If there are problems with the conception of fundamental theology as standing at the beginning of theological reflection, then what about the alternative of standing at the end? This view has been advanced by Raymond Pannikkar and Gerhard Ebeling, among others.[36] Both construe fundamental theology as primarily a meta-reflection on actual theological activity, with particular focus on the question of the truth of theology.[37] Obviously, this view is much closer to our own definition of fundamental theology. However, we would raise one minor objection. Too much emphasis on the place of fundamental theology at the end of theological reflection could suggest that such a discipline merely reflects on what has happened and has no influence on what is or will be. If fundamental theology is really concerned with legitimacy in theology, it must obviously reflect on how theology has actually been done. However, its goal is to influence how theology is and will be done. In view of this consideration, we would prefer to talk of fundamental theology being in a dialectical or circular relationship with the other theological disciplines. The question of where one would put a written account of the discipline in an actual theological encyclopedia is secondary to recognizing this actual circularity. We would put it at the end to avoid any suggestion that fundamental theology is something that can be done before or apart from the other moments of theological reflection.

A final example may help clarify our understanding of the placement of fundamental theology within theological reflection as a whole. David Tracy has recently presented an encyclopedic vision that divides theology into three distinct but related disciplines: fundamental theology, systematic theology and practical theology.[38] These disciplines are defined primarily by their relation to different "publics" which theology must address. Fundamental theology addresses primarily the academy; systematics, the church; and practical, society at large. How does this relate to our conception? The answer is suggested by considering Tracy's definition of fundamental theology. He sees the latter as concerned to provide arguments, which all reasonable persons would recognize as acceptable, for the basic questions of religion, God and Christ.[39] We see this task as belonging more to apologetics than to fundamental theology.

Accordingly, we would suggest that fundamental theology, as focused on insuring legitimacy in theology, is not one of the three alternatives that Tracy mentions, but rather a meta-reflection on all three. Support for this suggestion can be found in Tracy himself. He has found it desirable to divide both his work on fundamental theology and that on systematics into two parts.[40] The first part of each of these works deals primarily with what we would consider fundamental-theological matters.[41] By contrast, in the second part of *Blessed Rage* Tracy engages most actively in what we would consider apologetic argumentation.[42] We would suggest that his model in both books is first to give a fundamental-theological consideration of the methods and criteria of the discipline in question[43] and then to deal more closely with the actual content and structure of that discipline. If this is so, then *Blessed Rage* is not a fundamental theology per se. Rather, it is a fundamental-theological grounding of and a suggestive exemplification of a contemporary revisionist apologetic.

C. *Interconnection of Grounding Faith and Grounding Theology*

We noted in the introduction to this essay that fundamental theology is typically understood as a discipline that deals with questions of both the responsible justification of Christian faith (apologetics) and the methodological justification of Christian theology. In our historical survey of the discipline we saw how this association grew out of the "logic" of the discipline's development. We were, thereby, provided warrant for the argument that this association was not purely arbitrary and that a contemporary ecumenical fundamental theology should deal seriously with its claims. At the same time we noted, in both our historical and typological investigations, that this association is not without its tensions. For example, there have been continuing disagreements between those who view fundamental theology as primarily aimed at grounding faith (e.g., Fries, Rahner) and those who see it almost exclusively aimed at the methodological grounding of theology (e.g., Sauter).

We would agree with those who argue that the limitation of fundamental theology to either of these alternatives is an

unacceptable narrowing of the task and goal of the discipline.[44]
Therefore, we must comment briefly on how our understanding of
fundamental theology links together the tasks of grounding
faith and grounding theology.

An obvious point of connection between our conceptions of
grounding faith and grounding theology is the central role
that reflection on the world view of Christian faith plays in
each. Fundamental theology grounds faith inasmuch as it pro-
motes a critical self-understanding of this world view in
light of the possible objections to it. Reflection on the
world view of Christian faith plays a key role in fundamental
theology's attempts to ground theology as well. For example,
such reflection helps provide criteria for determining the
appropriateness of the sources, language and methods used in
theological formulations.

The crucial insight into the interconnection of the tasks
of grounding faith and grounding theology, however, is the
necessarily circular relationship between them. This can be
illustrated by two recent contrasting claims about the relationship of the apologetic task and questions of theological
method.[45] We noted earlier that Ted Peters articulated the
"logic" of the historical association of questions of theological method with those of apologetics in the claim that:
"If the proper 'road' or 'way' to ultimate truth (i.e.,
theological method) becomes available, then the apologetic
task will have been all but completed."[46] By contrast,
Matthias Neumann equally stresses the point that "the question
of ranking theological sources and the steps of theological
method can only become evident when the broader justifying
tasks of fundamental theology have been laid open and tra-
versed."[47] Our interest in these two claims is not to support
one over the other but rather, accepting both points as important, to argue for the necessary interrelationship of these
two types of reflection. Just as one cannot justify the
"content" of Christian theology without defending such things
as the methods and sources used in determining that content,
one cannot adequately defend these methods and sources without
giving attention to the question of their appropriateness to
theology's subject matter.

The same point can be made regarding our understanding of
how fundamental theology grounds faith and how it grounds
theology. The task of grounding faith by promoting a critical
self-understanding of the world view of Christian faith can
only be accomplished if it includes considerations of questions
on the sources, methods, language, etc., used in the theological
expression of that faith. At the same time, the task of
grounding theology by investigating the legitimacy of the
sources, methods, language, etc., utilized in theology must
take into consideration the subject matter with which the
former are intended to deal.

There is, thus, a necessary and creative interrelationship
between the task of grounding faith and that of grounding
theology. It is in light of this interrelationship that we
would defend the joining of these two basic tasks in the single
discipline of fundamental theology.

D. *Fundamental Theology and Extratheological Inquiry*

In our discussion so far we have made several brief references to the fact that fundamental theology has an important
relationship to extratheological inquiry. We must now
address this issue more directly.

Johannes Flury summarizes a widespread conviction about the
task and goal of fundamental theology when he describes one of
its primary functions as that of "providing a connection
between theology and society and science."[48] Before accepting
this characterization, we must clarify the directional nature
of the connection between fundamental theology and extratheological inquiry.

Elisabeth Gößmann expresses one possible understanding of
this connection when she asserts that fundamental theology has
the task of providing a scientific representation of theology
to those on the outside.[49] We find this understanding significantly deficient. Among other things, it suggests that the
importance of extratheological inquiry for fundamental theology
is limited merely to questions of the best form for presenting
an already established subject matter. The possibility that
the encounter with extratheological inquiry could lead to

alterations in the fundamental-theological understanding of
this subject matter is not taken into account.

Gottlieb Söhngen appears to be closer to the truth when he
assigns to fundamental theology the task of placing revelation
and theology before the claims of science *and* science before
the claims of revelation and theology.[50] That is, Söhngen sees
the relationship between fundamental theology and extratheological inquiry as being a two-way dialogue. Such a view
opens the possibility that fundamental theology can learn from
extratheological inquiry, as well as vice versa.

While appreciative of Söhngen's emphasis on the dialogical
character of the relationship between fundamental theology and
extratheological inquiry, we would modify this understanding
further through reflection on the goal of fundamental theology.
Fundamental theology is not the only theological discipline
in which the facilitation of dialogue between theology and
society or science plays a central role. In particular, this
activity plays a central role in apologetics as well. Bearing
in mind our distinction between the fundamental-theological
task of grounding faith and the apologetic task of recommending
or defending faith, we would argue that fundamental theology
is *primarily* interested in placing revelation and theology
before the claims of science while apologetics is *primarily*
interested in placing science before the claims of revelation
and theology. Obviously, as we have argued above, these two
concerns are not totally separable. Indeed, they function
best in a creative tension. Nonetheless, the fundamental
theologian's focus is on determining legitimacy *in* theology,
drawing whatever help he or she can from extratheological
inquiry into problems like the nature of human understanding,
while the apologist's focus is on defending both the content
of the critically established world view of Christian faith
and the right to existence of theology as a type of human
inquiry.

Thus, when fundamental theology is assigned the task of
providing a connection between theology and society or science,
it must be seen that the primary focus of this activity will
be on determining what contributions--both positive and nega-
tive--this extratheological inquiry can make to developing

a better critical self-understanding of the Christian faith
and the way in which theological expositions of that faith
are formulated.

The final question that must be clarified about the relationship of fundamental theology and extratheological inquiry
pertains to the scope of relevant extratheological disciplines.
Until recently, fundamental theology's extratheological discourse partner has usually been narrowly identified as
philosophy. This was possible because it was assumed that the
contribution of the other disciplines was mediated through
philosophy.[51] This assumption is now considered questionable.[52]
It is in this light that Geffré has argued that fundamental
theology will increasingly become the platform for the dialogue between faith and the human sciences and not only between
faith and philosophy as in the past.[53] To this we would add
that the contemporary fundamental theologian must also enter
into dialogue with other religions and ideologies.[54] In all
these areas, the focus of the discussion will be on achieving
a critically appraised understanding of Christian faith and
theology.

E. *Some Practical Considerations*

Further clarity about our understanding of fundamental
theology can be obtained by considering some of the practical
implications and issues related to it.

The first issue that must be considered pertains to the
relative distinctness of the discipline of fundamental theology. We have purposefully spoken of fundamental theology
more as a distinct "moment" in theological reflection than as
an isolated discipline. Our purpose in doing so was to avoid
two practical misconceptions. First, we do not see our proposal
as necessitating or even supporting the drastic separation of
the tasks of the fundamental theologian and the doctrinal
theologian or apologist, for example. It is likely and indeed
desirable that an individual theologian's interests and
expertise will bridge these distinct moments of theological
reflection. Likewise, we would not argue that the ideal procedure is to write a pure fundamental theology without
apologetic or dogmatic elements. Nonetheless, we do consider

encyclopedic clarity about the relative distinctness of the
various moments of theological reflection to be conducive to
the effective and legitimate functioning of theological
reflection.

The second practical consideration related to our understanding of fundamental theology pertains to the immensity of
its task and the practical impossibility of any one person
gaining mastery of its full scope. It is in light of this
practical problem that many fundamental theologians have begun
to urge that fundamental theology be handled by committee.[55]
Such cooperative work on the issues of fundamental theology
appears to be both inescapable and desirable. It must not,
however, obscure Rahner's point that fundamental theologians
must ultimately be willing to advance their own provisional
understandings of the subject matter of fundamental theology
as a whole.

The third practical consideration relates to the "time"
where a particular theologian should attempt to formulate
their fundamental-theological conceptions. There is a significant trend among contemporary theologians to try to resolve
fundamental-theological issues *prior* to engaging in constructive dogmatic reflection.[56] At the same time, strong protests
have been raised against this procedure, based both on historical precedents and procedural implications.[57] These
protesters usually advance the alternative of engaging in
fundamental-theological reflection only after dogmatic reflection. Our emphasis on the meta-reflective nature of
fundamental theology is more closely aligned to the latter
procedure. However, we would again emphasize the necessarily
circular relationship between constructive theological reflection and fundamental-theological reflection.

The final practical consideration is a didactic one: What
is the best place for teaching fundamental theology in a theological curriculum? Again, there have been proponents for
teaching it at the beginning and at the end. The most helpful
suggestion, however, conjoins these alternatives and proposes
that fundamental theology be taught in two parts.[58] At the
beginning of theological education there would be a provisional
fundamental-theological overview of the subject matter, sources,

and organization of theological reflection. Next would come
actual work in the various theological disciplines. Finally,
as a summation to theological education, there would be a
course which would give explicit consideration once more to
the various fundamental-theological issues, with particular
emphasis on the question of legitimacy in theological reflection as a whole. We believe such a procedure would bring
much needed clarity and organization to present theological
education.

F. *The Name "Fundamental Theology"*

One final issue that needs to be considered regarding our
proposed understanding of fundamental theology is the name
"fundamental theology" itself. Is this the most appropriate
name for the activity we have described? This question must
be considered from two perspectives. First, is this use of
the name "fundamental theology" sufficiently warranted by its
historical precedents? Second, are there alternative names
that might function better in the contemporary discussion of
these matters?

We will consider first the question of the historical
warrants for using "fundamental theology" to designate the
activity which we have described. The primary objection that
could be raised against our use of the term is that, whereas
fundamental theology has historically been identified or closely
associated with apologetics, we have carefully excluded
apologetics from the scope of the discipline we are proposing.
We would note two points in this regard. First, we have
shown that there is precedent in the modern discussion of
fundamental theology for distinguishing between an apologetic
task of grounding faith and a fundamental-theological task of
grounding faith. Second, and most importantly, one of the
strongest connecting threads of the various historical conceptions of fundamental theology is the close association of the
tasks of grounding faith and grounding theology (however these
are understood). This association is at the heart of our
proposal as well. Therefore, there appears to be sufficient
historical warrant for using this term.

Our choice of the name "fundamental theology" is also
prompted by the inadequacy of any alternative designations to
convey the task and scope of the "moment" of theological
reflection here under consideration. This can be seen by
considering several of these alternatives.

A common designation for a discipline that reflects on the
grounding of theology is "theological prolegomenon."[59] There
are two problems with this designation. First, it raises the
unacceptable suggestion that the tasks under consideration are
to be dealt with *prior* to actual theological reflection.
Second, in traditional Protestant usage this title has referred
primarily to an investigation that introduces dogmatics, whereas
we have argued for a view of fundamental theology as grounding
the larger theological enterprise.[60]

Another designation that has often been applied to investigations of the kind we have proposed is "philosophical
theology."[61] This designation has two significant shortcomings.
First, it has traditionally connoted an investigation and
defense of such basic questions as revelation and God on the
basis of reason alone, without drawing on the particulars of
Christian faith. We have explicitly rejected any such approach
as being neither possible nor helpful. Second, this designation appears to suggest that it embraces all uses of
philosophical reflection in theology. Such uses can hardly be
restricted to what we have distinguished as the task of
fundamental theology. They are equally important in doctrinal
formulations, ethics, etc.

An increasingly common designation which our emphasis on
the meta-reflective nature of fundamental theology would appear
to support is "metatheology."[62] Apart from its lack of
aesthetic appeal, the crucial problem with this designation is
the limitation of its most common definition. Raeburne
Heimbeck is representative when he defines it as "philosophical
theology in the age of analysis" and goes on to say its primary task is the logical analysis of the nature of religious
language.[63] While this is part of the task of our fundamental
theology, it is far from its total task.

Even if we accept the traditional German term *Fundamentaltheologie* as the most appropriate designation for the task

under consideration, we are still confronted with a choice
between two English translations: "foundational theology" and
"fundamental theology." Advocates for the alternative "foundational theology" have argued that "fundamental theology"
carries with it undesirable overtones of an apologetic or
natural theology.[64] While these dangers are real, it can also
be argued that "foundational theology" carries the undesirable
connotation of an extrinsic relationship between itself and
the rest of theology. Suggestive, in this regard, is Ebeling's
distinction between two possible emphases in talk about a
fundament. One can either mean that which is *merely the foundation* and not yet the building itself, or one can mean
something which is fundamental in the sense of the *decisive
factor* with which the building stands or falls.[65] "Foundational theology" tends to connote the first meaning while
"fundamental theology" carries more of the second (desirable)
emphasis. A further problem with the designation "foundational
theology" is that it has come to be identified with the particular formulation of Bernard Lonergan, which formulation we
have differentiated significantly from our own.

To be sure, each of the above alternatives could be refined
and used as a designation for the task we have defined.
Ultimately, then, our reasons for opting for "fundamental
theology" are reducible to two: First, there is significant
historical precedent for this use; second, "fundamental theology's" connotation of dealing with that which is essential
to theology best conveys our concern to locate the focus of
this "moment" of theological reflection in the question of
legitimacy in theology as a whole.

G. *Summary*

We noted at the beginning of part three that the essential
characteristic of an "ecumenical" fundamental theology would
be its ability to incorporate both the task of grounding faith
and that of grounding theology. In this chapter we have
attempted to clarify and defend an understanding of just such
an ecumenical fundamental theology. We focused this understanding of the discipline in the task of promoting a critical
self-understanding of the Christian faith among believers.

In the course of our clarification of this understanding
of fundamental theology, we were able to suggest its relationship to most of the positions treated in our typology of
the contemporary conceptions of fundamental theology. In
particular, we noted how each of the major approaches to
grounding faith could play a role in our understanding of
fundamental theology, provided that a distinction between
apologetic and fundamental-theological expressions of these
approaches is observed. We also assessed the possible incorporation of the various tasks assigned to a theological
grounding discipline in our ecumenical fundamental theology.[66]

---

[1] *Webster's Third New International Dictionary*, (Springfield, MA:
G & C Merriam, 1976), p. 1291.

[2] See Habermas, *Communication and the Evolution of Society*, (Boston:
Beacon Press, 1979). A good summary and analysis of this concept is avail-
able in Thomas McCarthy, *The Critical Theory of Jürgen Habermas*, (Cambridge,
MA: MIT Press, 1978), pp. 272-387. See also above, p. 128fn10.

[3] A good example is Pannenberg's detailed analysis and critical appropriation of the various positions in the discussion of the philosophy of
science.

[4] This illustration is drawn from the Catholic discussion where fundamental theology is explicitly considered. However, an essentially identical
distinction was advanced in Protestant circles which Gilkey has summarized
as one between an argumentative natural theology and an explicative prolegomenon to Christian theology. Cf. Gilkey, "Trends," pp. 154-55.

[5] E.g., Heinrich Fries, "Fundamental Theology," EnTh, p. 564: "Fundamental theology is the word now used for what used to be called apologetics.
This does not mean that the subject matter and goal of apologetics has been
abandoned, but that they have been made part of a more comprehensive theological reflection, primarily a positive one where apologetics plays a
decisive role, but is not the whole of fundamental theology." A Protestant
example of this type of answer would be Gilkey's replacement of natural
theology with the prolegomenon to Christian theology mentioned in the
previous footnote.

[6] Ibid., p. 547: "The task of fundamental theology is to describe
revelation."

[7] E.g., O'Collins, *Fundamental Theology*, pp. 23-24; Stirnimann, "Fundamentaltheologie," pp. 319-21; and Pannenberg, *Philosophy of Science*, p. 370.

[8] Implicit in this definition of apologetics is a differentiation between
even a primarily positive apologetic that tries to show how the meaning of
faith corresponds to human existence (e.g., Blondel) and fundamental theology per se, which concentrates more on understanding Christian faith than
on recommending it. The first understanding of the relationship of

fundamental theology and apologetics is not sufficiently cognizant of this distinction.

[9]Note in the latter regard that Stirnimann has argued that the distinction between fundamental theology per se and apologetics is a necessary prerequisite for Catholic theologians if they are to develop an ecumenical fundamental theology. Stirnimann, "Fundamentaltheologie," pp. 320-21.

[10]Cf. Alfred N. Whitehead, *Modes of Thought*, (NY: Free Press, 1968), pp. 48-50.

[11]Cf. above, p. 69.

[12]The distinction between these two types of grounding faith can be further clarified by considering the role of external criticism in each. For apologetics, external criticism is that which one must answer or refute, drawing on such resources as Christian tradition, doctrinal clarification or logical argumentation. By contrast, fundamental theology is not primarily concerned to respond to external criticism. Rather, it draws on external criticism as an aid in furthering its unique task of gaining a critical self-understanding of Christian faith.

[13]The question of how this task differs from the task of doctrinal theology will be considered in the next section of this chapter.

[14]Cf. O'Collins (*Fundamental Theology*, p. 23), who locates the central difference between fundamental theology and apologetics in the fact that the former presupposes faith while the latter cannot. This distinction could be misleading, however, if one took it to mean that apologetics does not appeal to the "content" of Christian faith in its arguments.

[15]We will use this same example later to distinguish fundamental theology from doctrinal theology.

[16]Cf., for example, our analyses of Tracy's *Blessed Rage* and Farley's *Ecclesial Man*. Pp. 74, 80-81, 87-88.

[17]Stirnimann argues the same point and considers its acceptance another prerequisite to the development of an ecumenical fundamental theology. Stirnimann, "Fundamentaltheologie," pp. 322-23.

[18]The importance of the fact that a critical reflection on the formal world view of Christian faith has been assigned to fundamental theology both in terms of its task of grounding faith and its task of grounding theology will be considered in the next section of this chapter.

[19]An explanation of our use of the designation "doctrinal theology" is in order. We have avoided the designation "systematic theology" because this term is normally understood as a comprehensive designation that embraces doctrinal theology, practical theology and perhaps even our fundamental theology (Cf. Ebeling, *Study of Theology*, p. 126; and Macquarrie, *Principles*, p. 39). "Dogmatic theology" has been rejected because, as Lonergan points out, it suggests a traditional approach to theology that was classicist in temperament. By contrast, "doctrinal theology" is more historically oriented since doctrinal formulations are understood to be context-determinate (Lonergan, *Methods*, p. 333).

[20]The following summary was suggested in part by an as-yet-unpublished article: Theodore W. Jennings, Jr., "The Vocation of the Theologian: The Construction of Doctrine."

[21]For example, Gerhard Ebeling determined in his fundamental-theological reflection on the subject matter of theology that theology explicates what can be asserted on the basis of 1) faith about the interrelatedness of the

experience of 2) God, 3) the world and 4) the self (Cf. *Study of Theology*, p. 162). He then used this fourfold scheme to organize his dogmatics. Cf. Ebeling, *Dogmatik des christlichen Glaubens*, (Tübingen: J.C.B. Mohr, 1979), I:73-75.

[22]Dietrich Bonhoeffer, *Letters and Papers from Prison*, (NY: Macmillan, 1962), pp. 164-65.

[23]Cf., for example, John A. T. Robinson's reflections on the place of worship and prayer in the absence of "religion." Robinson, *Honest to God*, (Phil.:   Westminster, 1963), pp. 84-104.

[24]Pesch, "Fundamentaltheologie und Dogmatik," esp. pp. 462ff.   Page numbers in this paragraph refer to this work.

[25]Stirnimann, "Fundamentaltheologie," p. 323.

[26]This is not to deny that a treatment of fundamental-theological issues would make a good introduction to theological education per se. See section E below for further discussion of this possibility.

[27]Cf. Joest, who uses this reason to reject the title "Prolegomenon to Dogmatics." Joest, *Fundamentaltheologie*, p. 10.

[28]Cf. Stirnimann, "Fundamentaltheologie," pp. 321-22.

[29]Cf. Joest, *Fundamentaltheologie*, p. 9.

[30]Cf. Flury, *Redlichkeit*, p. 295; and Ebeling, "Fundamentaltheologie," p. 164.

[31]Contra, Beintker, "Verstehen und Glauben," p. 296.

[32]Cf. George Lindbeck's analysis of Peukert: Lindbeck, "Theologische Methode und Wissenschaftstheorie," ThR 74 (1978):   273.

[33]Cf. above, pp. 123-24.

[34]E.g., Tracy, "Fundamental Theology as Contemporary Possibility," p. 14; and Lonergan, *Method*, p. 130.

[35]E.g., Rahner, *Hearers of the Word*, pp. 14-15.

[36]Pannikkar, "Metatheology," p. 47; and Ebeling, *Study of Theology*, p. 13.

[37]Pannikkar, "Metatheology," p. 48; and Ebeling, *Study of Theology*, p. 155.

[38]Tracy, *Analogical Imagination*, pp. 55-57.

[39]Cf. Tracy, *Analogical Imagination*, p. 57; and *idem*, "Defending the Public Character," p. 352.

[40]*Blessed Rage* and *Analogical Imagination*, respectively.   His work on practical theology has not yet been published.

[41]See Tracy's admission to this effect regarding the latter work: *Analogical Imagination*, p. 85fn31.

[42]Our summary of his *demonstratio religiosa* and *demonstratio christiana* draws entirely from this second section. Cf. above, pp. 74, 80-81.   Of course, even in this section we would have to distinguish between truly fundamental-theological concerns to clarify Christian faith and apologetic concerns to defend it.

[43]Cf. Tracy, "Theology as Public Discourse," p. 280.

[44]Cf.   Seckler, "Evangelische Fundamentaltheologie," p. 295; and Söhngen, "Fundamentaltheologie," pp. 1158-159.

[45]Though these claims are framed explicitly in terms of an apologetic conception of grounding faith, their basic point would remain true in terms of our description of the fundamental-theological task of grounding faith.

[46]Peters, "Truth in History," pp. 36-37.

[47]Neumann, "Imagination," p. 308fn3.

[48]Flury, *Redlichkeit*, p. 9fn11. Flury sees practical theology also fulfilling this function. He suggests that, due to this close connection with society, fundamental and practical theology will serve as a seismograph for theology as a whole--providing the first signs of an alienation from general consciousness.

[49]Gößmann, "Fundamentaltheologie," p. 48.

[50]Söhngen, "Fundamentaltheologie," p. 459.

[51]Cf. Tillich, *Systematic Theology I*, p. 18.

[52]Cf. Rahner, *Foundations*, p. 8.

[53]Geffré, "Recent Developments," p. 24.

[54]Cf. Stirnimann, "Evangelische Fundamentaltheologie," p. 379.

[55]Cf. Wagner, "Fundamentaltheologie," p. 26.

[56]Cf. Farley's two-part theological prolegomenon in *Ecclesial Man* and *Ecclesial Reflection*; and David Tracy's *Blessed Rage*, which was written prior to *Analogical Imagination*.

[57]Cf. Pesch, "Fundamentaltheologie und Dogmatik," p. 467, who sees this procedure as very unlike Luther or Aquinas; and Tillich, *Systematic Theology I*, p. 34, who argues that methodological awareness always follows the application of a method, it never precedes it.

[58]E.g., Latourelle, "Dismemberment," p. 40; and Stirnimann, "Fundamental-theologie," p. 361.

[59]E.g., Farley, *Ecclesial Reflection*, p. xiii; and Gilkey, *Naming*, pp. 232-35.

[60]For example, Brunner's Prolegomena deals with "The Basis and Task of Dogmatics." Brunner, *Doctrine of God*, p. 1.

[61]E.g. Macquarrie, *Principles*, p. 43.

[62]E.g., Pannikkar, "Metatheology," pp. 43-55.

[63]Raeburne Heimbeck, *Theology and Meaning*, (Stanford, CA: Stanford University Press, 1969), p. 19.

[64]E.g., Fiorenza, "Political Theology," p. 142.

[65]Ebeling, "Fundamentaltheologie," p. 511.

[66]We implicitly or explicitly incorporated all the tasks involved in insuring legitimacy *in* theology except that of developing the categories of theology (cf. above, p. 149, for our problem with the latter). To the extent that the demonstration of ways of insuring legitimacy *in* theology provides a basis for demonstrating the legitimacy *of* theology, the latter task is also incorporated into our discipline. However, we judged most of the explicit treatments of the legitimacy *of* theology to be exercises in apologetics, not fundamental theology.

CONCLUSION

FUNDAMENTAL THEOLOGY AND THEOLOGICAL METHOD

We began this essay by noting the stalemate that characterizes much of the contemporary discussion of questions of
theological method. Moreover, we suggested that a significant
reason for this stalemate was the lack of an accepted integrative context that could clarify the relationship of questions
of theological method with each other and with the theological
enterprise as a whole. At that point we suggested that a
promising move towards the creation of such an integrative
context was evident in the contemporary discussion of an ecumenical fundamental theology. We are now in a position to enlarge
on that suggestion by stating explicitly some of the advantages
that would be gained if questions of theological method could
come to be seen in the perspective of the larger task of an
ecumenical fundamental theology.

First, a recurring problem in discussions of theological
method is that they tend to focus on particular issues and to
lose sight of related problems. This can lead to two types of
distortion or deficiency: a) a failure to appreciate the contributions of other investigations to one's own problem, and
b) a failure to assess the implications of one's own investigations for related problems. One of the things that should
have become clear in our survey of the various investigations
involved in a fundamental theology that aims at grounding
theology is the way in which the individual investigations are
closely related to each other. For example, we have argued that
one cannot adequately determine the proper methods of theological investigation without considering the subject matter being
investigated. At the same time, an understanding of that
subject matter would entail considerations of such issues as
its sources and its linguistic nature. If questions of

167

theological method were investigated in the framework of an
ecumenical fundamental theology, the tendency to overlook
related issues may well be reduced.

Second, one of the reasons that it has been easy to overlook
related issues when investigating questions of theological
method is that there is no consensus on the scope of such
issues. Drawing on our typological investigation of the issues
involved in the fundamental-theological task of grounding theology, we would define its scope in terms of the questions of
the task and goal, subject matter, sources, language and unity
of theology. While our list may be inadequate, an attempt to
enlarge it will implicitly have adopted our concern to place
questions of theological method in a larger framework like
that of an ecumenical fundamental theology.

Finally, constructive consideration of questions of theological method can only take place when the horizon of such
questions is borne in mind. This horizon is the same as that
which we have identified in fundamental theology: the question
of legitimacy in the theological explication of Christian faith.
In light of our stress on the interrelationship of the various
aspects of fundamental theology, a theological formulation can
be considered legitimate ultimately only when it is shown to be
congruent with the task of theology, an expression or implication of the essential subject matter of theology, drawn from
the proper sources of theology through appropriate methods and
in light of the unity of theological reflection, and sensitive
to the linguistic levels of theology. We are not arguing that
one should postpone forwarding constructive theological proposals until all such questions are answered. However, we are
arguing that this full scope of questions becomes relevant when
the legitimacy of such a proposal becomes an issue.

In brief, the integration of questions of theological method
into the larger task of an ecumenical fundamental theology will
facilitate the central theological endeavor to more adequately
understand and articulate the Christian faith in the contemporary setting.

BIBLIOGRAPHY

A. Historical and Thematic Treatments of Fundamental Theology

Bouillard, Henri. "De l'Apologetique à la Théologie fondamentale." *Les quatre fleuves* 1 (1973): 57-70.

Cahill, Joseph. "A Fundamental Theology for our Time." *Concilium* 46 (1969): 93-101.

Crowe, Frederick. "Foundational Theology." NCE XVII, 235-37.

Dulles, Avery. "Fundamental Theology and the Dynamics of Conversion." *Thomist* 45 (1981): 175-93.

Ebeling, Gerhard. "Erwägungen zu einer evangelischen Fundamentaltheologie." ZThK 67 (1970): 479-524. Esp. pp. 479-509.

Eschweiler, Karl. *Die zwei Wege der neueren Theologie. Georg Heremes--Matthaias Joseph Scheeben.* Augsburg, 1926.

Flury, Johannes. *Um die Redlichkeit des Glaubens.* Freiburg: Freiburg Universität Verlag, 1979.

_____. "Was ist Fundamentaltheologie?" ThZ 31 (1975): 351-67.

Fries, Heinrich. "From Apologetics to Fundamental Theology." *Concilium* 46 (1969): 57-68.

_____. "Fundamental Theology." EnTh, 546-51.

_____. "Eine neue Fundamentaltheologie." ThQ 134 (1954): 458-76.

_____. "Die ökumenische Dimension der Fundamentaltheologie." *Ökumenische Rundschau* 22 (1973): 219-30.

_____. "Zum heutigen Stand der Fundamentaltheologie." TThZ 84 (1975): 351-63. Abbreviated English translation in ThD 24 (1976): 275-79.

Geffré, Claude. "Recent Developments in Fundamental Theology: An Interpretation." *Concilium* 46 (1969): 5-27.

Gilkey, Langdon. "Trends in Protestant Apologetics." *Concilium* 46 (1969): 125-57.

Gößmann, Elisabeth. "Fundamentaltheologie und Apologetik." In *Was ist Theologie?* Pp. 25-52. Edited by E. Neuhäusler and E. Gößmann. Munich: Max Heuber Verlag, 1966.

Hahn, Ferdinand. "Exegese und Fundamentaltheologie." ThQ 155 (1975): 262-80. Abbreviated English translation in ThD 24 (1976): 271-74.

Hill, William J. "Seeking Foundations for Faith: Symbolism of Person or Metaphysics of Being?" *Thomist* 45 (1981): 219-42.

Kolping, Adolf. "Zehn Jahre einer neuen Fundamentaltheologie." MThZ 15 (1964): 62-69.

Kolping, Adolf. *Fundamentaltheologie*. *Bd. I.* Münster: Regensberg Verlag, 1968. Pp. 35-70.

Latourelle, René. "Dismemberment or Renewal of Fundamental Theology?" *Concilium* 46 (1969): 29-41.

Lehmann, Karl. "Apologetik und Fundamentaltheologie." InKaZ 7 (1978): 289-94.

Metz, Johann Baptist, ed. *The Development of Fundamental Theology*. Volume 46 of *Concilium*. NY: Seabury, 1969.

Neumann, Matthias. "The Role of Imagination in the Tasks of Fundamental Theology." Enc 42 (1981): 307-27.

Nitzschke, K. "Fundamentaltheologie." EKL I, 1408.

Pesch, Otto. "Fundamentaltheologie und Dogmatik, Erwägungen zu einer unvermeidlichen aber problematischen Unterscheidung." In *Unterwegs zur Einheit*, pp. 445-75. Edited by J. Brantschen and P. Selvatico. Freiburg: Herder, 1980.

Petri, Heinrich. "Die Entdeckung der Fundamentaltheologie in der evangelischen Theologie." *Catholica* 33 (1979): 241-61.

_____. "Fundamentaltheologie im Umbau." ThGl 69 (1979): 95-105.

Pannikkar, Raymond. "Metatheology or Diacritical Theology as Fundamental Theology." *Concilium* 46 (1969): 43-55.

Platzer, F. "Zu einem Entwurf der Fundamentaltheologie." *Theologie der Gegenwart* 18 (1975): 165-70.

Schmitz, Josef. "Die Fundamentaltheologie im 20. Jahrhundert." In *Bilanz der Theologie im 20. Jahrhundert*, pp. 197-245. Edited by H. Vorgrimler and R. Vander Gucht. Freiburg: Herder, 1969.

Seckler, Max. "Evangelische Fundamentaltheologie. Zu einem Novum aus katholischer Sicht." ThQ 155 (1975): 281-99.

Seiterich, E. *Wege der Glaubensbegründung nach der sogennanten Immanenzapologetik*. Freiburg: Herder, 1938.

Segundo, Juan Luis. "Fundamental Theology and Dialogue." *Concilium* 46 (1969): 69-79.

Shea, William M. "The Stance and Task of the Foundational Theologian: Critical or Dogmatic?" HeyJ 17 (1976): 273-92.

Söhngen, Gottlieb. "Wunderzeichen und Glaube. Biblische Grundlegung der katholischen Apologetik." In *Die Einheit der Theologie*, pp. 265-85. Munich: K. Zink Verlag, 1952.

Stakemeier, Eduard. "Zur Heilsgeschichtlichen Orientierung der Fundamentaltheologie nach dem Zweiten Vatikanum." *Catholica* 21 (1967): 101-126.

Stirnimann, Heinrich. "Evangelische Fundamentaltheologie." FZPhTh 22 (1975): 375-83.

_____. "Erwägungen zur Fundamentaltheologie. Problematik, Grundfragen, Konzept." FZPhTh 24 (1977): 291-323.

VanderMark, William. "Fundamental Theology: A Bibliographical and Critical Survey." RelStR 8 (1982): 244-53.

Verweyan, Hansjürgen. "Fundamentaltheologie - Hermeneutik - Erste Philosophie." ThPh 56 (1981): 358-88.

Wagner, Harald. "Evangelische Fundamentaltheologie." *Catholica* 31 (1977):
    17-28.

Walgrave, Jan. "The Essence of Modern Fundamental Theology." *Concilium*
    46 (1969): 81-91.

B. Contemporary Fundamental-Theological Investigations

Apczynski, John. "Integrative Theology: A Polanyian Proposal for Theo-
    logical Foundations." TS 40 (1979): 23-43.

Beintker, Horst. "Verstehen und Glauben: Grundlinien einer evangelischen
    Fundamentaltheologie." KuD 22 (1976): 22-40.

Biser, Eugen. *Glaubensverständnis. Grundriss einer hermeneutischen
    Fundamentaltheologie.* Freiburg: Herder, 1975.

Bouillard, Henri. "Human Experience as the Starting Point of Fundamental
    Theology." *Concilium* 6 (1965): 79-91.

_____. *The Logic of Faith.* New York: Sheed & Ward, 1967.

_____. "La Tâche actuelle de la Théologie fondamentale." *Le Point
    Théologique* 2 (1972): 7-49.

Darlap, Adolf. "Fundamentaltheologie des Heilsgeschichte." *Mysterium
    Salutis*, Vol. I, pp. 3-256. Einsiedeln: Benziger Verlag, 1965.

Dolch, Heimo. "Der systematische Ort der Kirche. Zur Frage des Ausgangs-
    punktes und der Methode der Fundamentaltheologie." In *Volk Gottes.
    Festgabe für J. Höfer*, pp. 28-40. Freiburg: Herder, 1967.

Ebeling, Gerhard. "Erwägungen zu einer evangelischen Fundamentaltheologie."
    ZThK 67 (1970): 479-524.

_____. *God and Word.* Philadelphia, PA: Fortress, 1967.

_____. "Hermeneutische Theologie?" In *Wort und Glaube II*, pp. 99-120.
    Tübingen: J.C.B. Mohr, 1969.

_____. *Introduction to a Theological Theory of Language.* Philadelphia,
    PA: Fortress, 1973.

_____. "Reflections on Speaking Responsibly of God." In *Word and Faith*,
    pp. 333-53. Philadelphia, PA: Fortress, 1963.

_____. *The Study of Theology.* Philadelphia, PA: Fortress, 1978.

_____. "Theology and the Evidentness of the Ethical." JThC 2 (1965):
    96-129.

Farley, Edward. *Ecclesial Man.* Philadelphia, PA: Fortress, 1975.

_____. *Ecclesial Reflection.* Philadelphia, PA: Fortress, 1982.

Fiorenza, Francis. "Political Theology as Foundational Theology." *The
    Catholic Theological Society of America. Proceedings of the 32nd
    Annual Convention* (1977): 142-77.

Gelpi, Donald L. *Experiencing God.* New York: Paulist, 1978.

Gilkey, Langdon. *Naming the Whirlwind.* Indianapolis, IN: Bobbs Merrill,
    1969.

_____. *Reaping the Whirlwind.* New York: Seabury, 1976.

_____. *Society and the Sacred.* New York: Crossroad, 1981.

Grabner-Haider, Anton. *Theorie der Theologie als Wissenschaft*. Munich: Kösel Verlag, 1974.

Hart, Ray L. *Unfinished Man and the Imagination*. New York: Seabury, 1968.

Hilberath, Bernd Jochen. *Theologie zwischen Tradition und Kritik*. Düsseldorf: Patmos, 1975.

Jeffner, Anders. *Kriterien christlichen Glaubenslehre*. Uppsala: Upsaliensis Acadamiae, 1977.

Jennings, Theodore W., Jr. *Introduction to Theology*. Philadelphia, PA: Fortress, 1976.

Joest, Wilfried. *Fundamentaltheologie. Theologische Grundlagen und Methodenprobleme*. Stuttgart: Kohlhammer, 1974.

Kaufmann, Gordon D. *An Essay on Theological Method*. Missoula, MT: Scholar's Press, 1975.

Knauer, Peter. *Der Glaube kommt vom Hören: Ökumenische Fundamentaltheologie*. Cologne: Styria, 1977.

Kolping, Adolf. *Fundamentaltheologie. Bd. I, Theorie der Glaubwürdigkeitserkenntnis der Offenbarung* (1968). *Bd. II, Die konkretgeschichtliche Offenbarung Gottes* (1974). *Bd. III, Die katholische Kirche als Sachwalterin der Offenbarung Gottes. I. Teil: Die geschichtlichen anfänge der Kirche Christi* (1981). Münster: Regensberg Verlag.

Lonergan, Bernard. *Method in Theology*. New York: Seabury, 1972.

Macquarrie, John. *Principles of Christian Theology*. New York: Scribner's, 1966. Pp. 1-174.

_____. "The Problem of Natural Theology." In *Thinking About God*, pp. 132-41. New York: Harper and Row, 1975.

Metz, Johann Baptist. *Faith in History and Society: Towards a Practical Fundamental Theology*. New York: Seabury, 1980.

Micskey, Koloman. *Die Axiom-Syntax des evangelischen dogmatischen Denkens*. Göttingen: Vandenhoeck and Ruprecht, 1976.

Monden, Louis. *Faith: Can Man Still Believe?* New York: Sheed & Ward, 1970.

Nygren, Anders. *Meaning and Method*. Philadelphia, PA: Fortress, 1972.

O'Collins, Gerald. *Fundamental Theology*. New York: Paulist, 1981.

Ogden, Schubert. *The Reality of God*. New York: Harper and Row, 1963.

_____. "The Task of Philosophical Theology." In *The Future of Philosophical Theology*, pp. 55-84. Edited by Robert Evans. Philadelphia, PA: Westminster, 1971.

_____. "What is Theology?" JR 52 (1972): 22-40.

Ott, Heinrich. "What is Systematic Theology?" In *The Later Heidegger and Theology*, pp. 77-111. Edited by J. M. Robinson and J. B. Cobb. New York: Harper and Row, 1963.

Pannenberg, Wolfhart. *Ethics*. Philadelphia, PA: Westminster, 1981.

_____. *The Idea of God and Human Freedom*. Philadelphia, PA: Westminster, 1973.

_____. *Theology and the Philosophy of Science*. Philadelphia, PA: Westminster, 1976.

Pannenberg, Wolfhart. *What is Man?* Philadelphia, PA: Fortress, 1970.

Peukert, Helmut. *Wissenschaftstheorie - Handlungstheorie - Fundamentaltheologie.* Düsseldorf: Suhrkamp, 1976.

Rahner, Karl. "Formal und Fundamentaltheologie." LThK[2] IV, 205-6.

_____. *Foundations of Christian Faith.* New York: Seabury, 1978.

_____. "Fundamental Theology." In *Theological Dictionary*, pp. 181-82. Edited by K. Rahner and H. Vorgrimler. New York: Herder, 1965.

_____. *Hearers of the Word.* New York: Seabury, 1969.

_____. "The Prospects for Dogmatic Theology." *Theological Investigations I*, pp. 1-18. New York: Seabury, 1961.

_____. "Reflections on the Contemporary Intellectual Formation of Future Priests." *Theological Investigations VI*, pp. 113-38. New York: Seabury, 1969.

_____. "Reflections on a New Task for Fundamental Theology." *Theological Investigations XVI*, pp. 156-66. New York: Seabury, 1979.

_____. "A Scheme for a Treatise of Dogmatic Theology." *Theological Investigations I*, pp. 19-37. New York: Seabury, 1961.

Sauter, Gerhard, *et al.* *Grundlagen der Theologie--ein Diskurs.* Stuttgart: Kohlhammer, 1974.

Sauter, Gerhard. *Wissenschaftstheoretische Kritik der Theologie.* Munich: Christian Kaiser Verlag, 1973.

Schillebeeckx, Eduard. *Revelation and Theology.* London: Sheed & Ward, 1967.

_____. "Towards a Catholic Use of Hermeneutics." In *God the Future of Man*, pp. 3-49. New York: Sheed & Ward, 1968.

_____. *The Understanding of Faith.* New York: Seabury, 1974.

Schupp, Franz. *Auf dem Weg zu einer kritischen Theologie.* Freiburg: Herder, 1974.

Söhngen, Gottlieb. "Fundamentaltheologie." LThK[2] IV, 452-59.

Stirnimann, Heinrich. "Erwägungen zur Fundamentaltheologie. Problematik, Grundfragen, Konzept." FZPhTh 24 (1977): 291-365.

Tracy, David. *The Analogical Imagination.* New York: Crossroad, 1981.

_____. *Blessed Rage for Order.* New York: Seabury, 1975.

_____. "Defending the Public Character of Theology." *Christian Century* 98 (1981): 350-56.

_____. "Foundational Theology as a Contemporary Possibility." *Dunwoodie Review* 12 (1972): 3-20.

_____. "Theology as Public Discourse." *Christian Century* 92 (1975): 280-84.

Wagner, Harald. *Einführung in die Fundamentaltheologie.* Darmstadt: Wissenschaftliche Buchgesellschaft, 1981.

C. Other Sources Cited

Adam, Karl. *Glaube und die Glaubewissenschaften*. Rottenburgln, 1923.

Aland, Kurt. *Apologie der Apologetik*. Berlin: Walter de Gruyter, 1948.

Anderson, Wilhelm. *Der Gesetzbegriff in der gegenwärtigen theologischen Diskussion. Überlegungen zu Gerhard Ebeling*. Munich: Christian Kaiser Verlag, 1963.

Aubert, Rogert. *Le Problème de l'acte de foi*. Louvain: Warney, 1950.

Barth, Karl. *Anselm. Fides Quarens Intellectum*. London: SCM Press, 1960.

_____. *Church Dogmatics I:1*. Edinburgh: T & T Clark, 1975.

Bayer, Oswald. *Was ist das: Theologie?* Stuttgart: Calwer Verlag, 1973.

Birkner, H. J. "Natürliche Theologie und Offenbarungs Theologie." NZSTh 3 (1961): 279-95.

Blondel, Maurice. *The Letter on Apologetics, and History and Dogma*. New York: Holt, Rinehart and Winston, 1968.

Bonhoeffer, Dietrich. *Letters and Papers from Prison*. New York: Macmillan, 1962.

Brunner, Emil and Barth, Karl. *Natural Theology*. London: Centenary Press, 1946.

Brunner, Emil. "Die andere Aufgabe der Theologie." ZZ (1929): 255-76.

_____. *The Christian Doctrine of God*. Philadelphia, PA: Westminster, 1950.

Cobb, John B. *Living Options in Protestant Theology*. Philadelphia, PA: Westminster, 1962.

_____. "Review of David Tracy's *The Analogical Imagination*." RelStR 7 (1981): 281-84.

Daiber, Karl-Fritz. "Helmut Peukert's *Wissenschaftstheorie - Handlungstheorie - Fundamentaltheologie*." EvTh 38 (1978): 444-50.

Dulles, Avery. *A History of Apologetics*. Philadelphia, PA: Westminster, 1971.

_____. "Method in Fundamental Theology: Reflections on David Tracy's *Blessed Rage for Order*." TS 37 (1976): 304-16.

Ebeling, Gerhard. *Dogmatik des christlichen Glaubens I*. Tübingen: J.C.B. Mohr, 1979.

Eberhard, Kenneth. *Karl Rahner's Doctrine of the Supernatural Existential*. Ann Arbor, MI: University Microfilms, 1971.

Ehrlich, Johann Nepomuk. *Fundamentaltheologie*. 2 vols. Prague, 1859-1862.

Ferré, Nels F. S. *Swedish Contributions to Modern Theology*. New York: Harper and Row, 1967.

Gadamer, Hans Georg. *Truth and Method*. New York: Seabury, 1975.

Gardeil, Ambrose. *Le donné révelé et la théologie*. Paris: Gabalda, 1910.

Geffré, Claude. *A New Age in Theology*. New York: Paulist, 1974.

Geiselmann, Joseph. *Die katholischer Tübinger Schule*. Freiburg: Herder, 1964.

Gerhard, Johann. *Loci Theologici*. Edited by Eduard Preuss, 1893.

Grotius, Hugo. *The Truth of the Christian Religion*. Translated by John Clark. London: J & P Knapton, 1829.

Gutiérrez, Gustavo. *A Theology of Liberation*. Maryknoll, NY: Orbis, 1973.

Habermas, Jürgen. *Communication and the Evolution of Society*. Boston: Beacon Press, 1979.

_____. *Knowledge and Human Interests*. Boston: Beacon Press, 1972.

Heimbeck, Raeburne. *Theology and Meaning*. Stanford, CA: Stanford University Press, 1969.

Hodgson, Peter. *New Birth of Freedom*. Philadelphia, PA: Fortress, 1976.

Kaufman, Gordon D. "Review of Farley's *Ecclesial Man*." RelStR 2:4 (1976): 10-13.

Kelsey, David. "The Bible and Christian Theology." JAAR 48 (1980): 385-402.

_____. *The Uses of Scripture in Recent Theology*. Philadelphia, PA: Fortress, 1975.

Kirk, J. Andrew. *Liberation Theology*. Atlanta, GA: John Knox, 1979.

Knauer, Peter. "Review of Wilfried Joest's *Fundamentaltheologie*." ThPh 51 (1976): 607-9.

Lammiman, Forrest. "Theology and Theories of Language." Enc 33 (1972): 400-10.

Lang, Albert. *Fundamentaltheologie*. Bd. I, *Die Sendung Christi* (1953). Bd. II, *Der Auftrag der Kirche* (1962). Munich: Max Heuber Verlag.

Lindbeck, George. "Theologische Methode und Wissenschaftstheorie." ThR 74 (1978): 265-80.

Lonergan, Bernard. *Insight. A Study of Human Understanding*. New York: Harper and Row, 1958.

McCarthy, Thomas. *The Critical Theory of Jürgen Habermas*. Cambridge, MA: MIT Press, 1978.

McCool, Gerald. *Catholic Theology in the Nineteenth Century*. New York: Seabury, 1977.

Mann, Erwin. *Idee und Wirklichkeit der Offenbarung. Method und Aufbau der Fundamentaltheologie des Güntherianers J. N. Ehrlich*. Vienna: Verband der wissenschaften Gesellschaften Österreichs, 1977.

Maritain, Jacques. *The Angelic Doctor*. New York: Dial Press, 1931.

Metz, Johann Baptist. "Apologetics." EnTh pp. 20-24.

_____. "Political Theology." EnTh pp. 1238-43.

Moltmann, Jürgen. "The Revelation of God and the Question of Truth." In *Hope and Planning*, pp. 3-30. New York: Harper and Row, 1971.

_____. *Theology of Hope*. New York: Harper and Row, 1967.

_____. "Towards a Political Hermeneutic of the Gospel." In *Religion, Revolution and the Future*, pp. 83-107. New York: Scribner's, 1969.

O'Brein, William J. "A Methodological Flaw in Tracy's Revisionist Theology." *Horizons* 5 (1978): 175-84.

Rahner, Karl. "Some Critical Reflections on 'Functional Specialties in Theology'." In *Foundations in Theology*, pp. 194-96. Edited by Philip McShane. Notre Dame, IN: University of Notre Dame Press, 1971.

Reardon, Bernard. *Liberalism and Tradition*. Cambridge: Cambridge University Press, 1975.

Ricoeur, Paul. *Main Trends in Philosophy*. New York: Holmes and Meier, 1979.

Robbins, J. Wesley. "Professor Gilkey and Alternative Methods of Theological Construction." JR 52 (1972): 84-101.

Robinson, John A. T. *Honest to God*. Philadelphia, PA: Westminster, 1963.

Rousselot, Pierre. *The Intellectualism of Saint Thomas*. London: Sheed & Ward, 1935.

_____. "Les Yeux de la Foi." RSR 1 (1910): 241-59, 444-75.

Santoni, Ronald, ed. *Religious Language and the Problem of Religious Knowledge*. Bloomington, IN: Indiana University Press, 1968.

Schleiermacher, D. Friedrich. *Brief Outline of the Study of Theology*. Richmond, VA: John Knox, 1966.

_____. *The Christian Faith*. Philadelphia, PA: Fortress, 1976.

Schlochtern, Josef Meyer zu. "Verständingung über den Glauben. Anmerkungen zu Bisers Fundamentaltheologie." TThZ 85 (1976): 344-56.

Schoof, T. Mark. *A Survey of Catholic Theology--1800-1970*. New York: Paulist and Newman Press, 1970.

Segundo, Juan Luis. *The Liberation of Theology*. Maryknoll, NY: Orbis, 1976.

Siebert, Rudolf J. "Peukert's New Critical Theology." *The Ecumenist* 16 (1977): 52-58, 78-80.

Sölle, Dorothee. *Political Theology*. Philadelphia, PA: Fortress, 1974.

Szekeres, Attila. "Karl Barth und die natürliche Theologie." EvTh 24 (1964): 229-42.

Tillich, Paul. *Systematic Theology I*. Chicago, IL: University of Chicago Press, 1951.

Torrance, Thomas. *Theological Science*. Oxford: Oxford University Press, 1969.

Tracy, David. "Lonergan's Foundational Theology: An Interpretation and Critique." In *Foundations in Theology*, pp. 197-222. Edited by Philip McShane. Notre Dame, IN: University of Notre Dame Press, 1971.

Whitehead, Alfred North. *Modes of Thought*. New York: Free Press, 1968.

Zahrnt, Heinz. *The Question of God*. New York: Harcourt, Brace and World, 1969.

INDEX OF PRINCIPAL NAMES

177